LEAVE IT BETTER THAN
YOU FOUND IT

John Nordstrom, Jack McMillan, Jim Nordstrom, and Bruce Nordstrom in 1971

LEAVE IT BETTER THAN YOU FOUND IT

Bruce A. Nordstrom

DOCUMENTARY MEDIA

SEATTLE, WASHINGTON

LEAVE IT BETTER THAN YOU FOUND IT

First edition 2007

Printed in Canada

Documentary Media LLC
3250 41st Avenue S.W.
Seattle, Washington 98116
206 935-9292
www.documentarymedia.com

Library of Congress Cataloging-in-Publication Data

Nordstrom, Bruce A., 1933–
Leave it better than you found it / Bruce A. Nordstrom.

p. cm.

Includes index.

ISBN-13: 978-1-933245-05-8

1. Nordstrom (Firm)—History. 2. Department stores—United States—History. 3. Family-owned business enterprises—United States—Case studies. 4. Nordstrom, Bruce A., 1933– 5. Businesspeople—United States—Biography. I. Title.

HF5465.U6N676 2007
381'.1410973—dc22

2007007451

This book is dedicated to my wife, Jeannie

TABLE OF CONTENTS

Bruce Nordstrom

INTRODUCTION

In 1950, my grandfather John W. Nordstrom wrote his autobiography, entitled *The Immigrant in 1887*. He began, "I am writing this for my grandchildren to read after I am gone, to let them know what the average immigrant had to go through in the 1880s. Not that it was any worse for me than a lot of others, but after reading this they should be happy that they were born in America."

As one of his grandchildren, I was lucky enough not only to read that book while he was still alive (he passed away in 1963, at the age of 92) but also to know him well and love him dearly.

Grandpa's book detailed his hardscrabble life in Sweden, his migration to America at age 16, and his struggles to gain a foothold in this country. He held many jobs — laborer, logger, farmer, coal and silver miner, and gold prospector — until he made his "fortune," about $13,000, during the Gold Rush of the late 1890s.

After the Gold Rush, Grandpa returned to Seattle, where he renewed his acquaintance with Carl F. Wallin, whom he had first met as a fellow gold prospector in the Klondike. By this time, Wallin was operating a tiny shoe-repair shop on Fourth Avenue and Pike Street. The two men decided to form a partnership and, in 1901, they opened a shoe store called Wallin & Nordstrom, at the same location. As the young city of Seattle grew up around them, they built a successful little shoe store.

In 1985, my uncle Elmer, the last surviving son of John W., wrote a book called *A Winning Team: The Story of Everett, Elmer & Lloyd Nordstrom*, in which he described how he and his brothers took over the business from Grandpa and Carl Wallin and built the biggest independent shoe retailer in the United States.

I am a representative of the third generation of Nordstroms, and it's my turn to write about what transpired in the years that I worked with my cousins John and Jim Nordstrom and my cousin-by-marriage Jack McMillan.

With the benefit of the research capabilities of our Nordstrom corporate staff, this book sets the factual record straight in terms of specific dates, numbers, and events in the history of our company.

The reader should note that I am describing the events that transpired on our watch from my own point of view, which might (and probably does) differ somewhat from that of my cousins.

As the reader will discover, this is more than just a book about the company that I love. It is also the story of my own life and the people who made it a special one.

My grandfather, Nordstrom founder John W. Nordstrom, and my grandmother Hilda at their cabin on Hood Canal

CHAPTER I

GROWING UP

I was born at Seattle General Hospital on October 1, 1933, to Everett and Libby Nordstrom, a Depression baby with a capital D. Two and a half years later, my sister, Anne, was born. Growing up, I wondered why my parents had only two kids. I guess the primary reason was that they weren't making much money in those days, so Anne and I were lucky that either one of us was born.

I grew up in the Montlake neighborhood of Seattle, on Hamlin Street, right across the canal from the University of Washington. When my folks were first married, their goal was to make $10,000 a year, which was pretty good money back in those days. They paid $6,000 to buy a nice white Colonial-style home on a pretty little street, where we lived for 12 years. They sold it for $12,000, doubling their investment. Today, that same house is worth about half a million dollars, which is a small indication of how Seattle has changed since I was a kid.

My grandpa John W. Nordstrom, who lived five doors from us, was a modest, very Swedish immigrant for whom life was just fine. His attitude was that you take life as it comes; whatever happens happens. I loved him so much. To his young grandchildren, he was a sweet, mild-mannered, always-smiling man who didn't have a mean bone in his body. But when I read his memoir and asked him questions, I was shocked to learn what a tough life he'd had, and how he'd had the guts, the perseverance, and the stick-to-itiveness to prevail over terrible adversity. As an older man, he was a gentle soul, but in his youth, he had obviously needed incredible toughness and fortitude just to make the thousand-mile journey from Seattle to the Klondike (he had to slaughter his horse for food), let alone to survive for two years as a struggling gold prospector.

My father and uncles didn't want to just run a shoe store; they wanted to run the biggest and the best shoe store there was.

Our family, around 1940

In our conversations, Grandpa didn't talk about the shoe store very much, but I soon became aware that it was his business, and it was his initiative that had started it.

After Grandpa made his money in the Yukon, he returned to Seattle, where, as he wrote in his memoir, "I renewed my acquaintance with a girl I had taken out a few times before going to Alaska." Her name was Hilda Carlson, and coincidentally, she came from Grandpa's hometown of Luleå, a small farming community in the northernmost part of Sweden, 60 miles below the Arctic Circle. Ironically, they had not known each other in Luleå. Hilda was a housemaid for one of the rich families in Seattle, and when Grandpa came to court her, he had to visit her through the servants' entrance.

Grandma was as sweet as grandmothers usually are, but to me, she was the tougher of the two, the one who wore the pants in the family. She was fiercely loyal to our company. When she found out that her milkman bought his shoes at Sears, she switched dairies.

I went to Montlake grade school and Meany Junior High School, and was all set to attend Garfield High School when my parents sold our house and we moved out to the north end of Seattle. So instead of attending Garfield with all my friends, I enrolled at Roosevelt High School, which was the biggest high school in the state. For a 15-year-old kid, that is a very traumatic time to suddenly be taken out of your comfort zone. I did not know one person at Roosevelt, and until I started making friends, I was very unhappy.

One of the first people I met was Blake Eagle, who became my best pal throughout high school and later at the University of Washington. Although we didn't belong to the same fraternity, his fraternity house was right across the street from mine, so we still saw a lot of each other. When Fran Wakeman and I married in 1959, Blake was my best man, and when my first son was born, we named him after Blake. When both of our families were living on Mercer Island, Blake coached my boys in many sports, and we remained close friends with him and his wife, Jane. Blake, who has had many important jobs, became an expert in commercial real estate and was recruited by the Massachusetts Institute of Technology to start their school of commercial real estate. Blake and I were only average students, so it just goes to show you that real-world experience is often more valuable than a formal education.

My grandfather John W. Nordstrom with his three sons — my uncle Lloyd, my father, Everett, and my uncle Elmer

THE FAMILY SHOE STORE

From the time I was old enough to understand such things, I knew that my father and my uncles, Elmer and Lloyd, owned a couple of shoe stores — one in downtown Seattle, by then on Second Avenue and Pike Street, and a second store on University Avenue, near the University of Washington.

Everett and Elmer, the oldest Nordstrom boys, grew up in the business; they both began working in the store at age 12. In 1923, when Wallin & Nordstrom opened the store in the University District, Everett, who had just graduated from the UW Business School at the age of 20, was put in charge of the opening.

By the mid-1920s, the relationship had soured between Mr. Wallin and Grandpa, who wrote in his book, "The business seemed to be going backward instead of going ahead, and I was not happy as we did not seem to agree on anything." Elmer would later write in his book that Mr. Wallin "had resented us coming into the store when we were young. I remember one time, it was a Fourth of July or a big day, I was maybe 12 years old. My dad said, 'Why don't you come down; you could sell shoe polish or maybe run some errands around the front of the store.' I remember walking in with him, and Mr. Wallin said, 'What's he doing here? We don't need him.' I had to go home. That was kind of rough. But then in later years, as we got older, that never happened."

In 1928, Grandpa convinced my dad and Uncle Elmer, who at the time were 25 and 24, respectively, to buy his interest in the company. A year later, a somewhat reluctant Mr. Wallin sold his share to them as well. At the time, Lloyd was still an undergraduate at the UW. He didn't join his brothers in the business until after he graduated, in 1932.

Mr. Wallin vacationed in a log cabin on Hood Canal, right next door to my grandfather's summer place. When I knew him, he was an old man, with white, white hair, and he was kind of intimidating because he didn't smile a lot. My cousins and I were a bunch of kids running around the property, and he wasn't thrilled with that. When I became older, I realized that, as far as our family was concerned, the important thing about Carl Wallin was that he introduced us Nordstroms to the shoe business.

My dad and uncles bought the business just in time for the Great Depression, but with typical drive and ambition, they confronted adversity and forged ahead. In 1930, they renovated the Second Avenue store by tripling the display and merchandising area, replacing the linoleum with carpeting, improving the lighting with new chandeliers and fixtures, and installing comfortable upholstered chairs that blended with the soft tones of the silver-gray oak cabinet work. That year, they changed the name of the company to Nordstrom's.

In 1937, with their lease about to expire, the brothers decided to build a store on Fifth Avenue between Pike and Pine Streets, on the site of the old Owl Drugstore. This was not a very popular decision with my grandfather because back then, Fifth and Pike was on the periphery of the downtown business core. Frederick & Nelson and The Bon Marché were there, but not much else. Of course, that area eventually became the retail center of downtown, and we remained in that location for the next 61 years.

Making the move even riskier was the fact that the country was still deeply mired in the Depression. Nevertheless, the brothers were gutsy, confident guys who seized opportunities. With the business thriving at the new location, they enlarged the store by expanding into the building next door. The expansion strapped them for cash, but they were committed to achieving their goal of being the largest shoe store in town.

When I think back on their courage, I'm amazed. Everett, Elmer, and Lloyd came from humble immigrant parents who didn't have much in the way of material things but did instill in their children a work ethic, fearlessness, and an ambition to succeed.

Interestingly, the brothers were conservative in their personal lives, buying only modest, affordable houses and automobiles. But when it came to the business, they rolled the dice because they had a concept that they really believed in.

My father and uncles didn't want to just run a shoe store; they wanted to run the biggest and the best shoe store there was. Okay, then how do you get there in a medium-sized town like Seattle? The answer: Sell shoes to everybody in town. That means you've got to stock as many sizes, styles, colors, and brands as you can, i.e., kill 'em with inventory. Their strategy was to build bigger stores, display nice windows, and hire better help. They lifted the bar for every shoe retailer, especially themselves.

My father and uncles, who focused on the great middle market, were (as Nordstrom still is today) very value-oriented. Our philosophy is that whatever the retail price — back then, the average price for a shoe at Nordstrom was less than $10 — we must offer a good value.

By the time I was aware of things, they had achieved their goal. We were a big shoe store, by far the biggest shoe seller in town.

When I was four or five years old, my dad would take me downtown on Sundays when they were building the new Nordstrom store at Fifth Avenue and Pike Street. Back then, the store wasn't open on Sundays, so while Dad did his office work, I would play among the construction sawhorses.

When I think back on their courage,

I'm amazed.

My first memory of being connected in some funny way to a shoe store was sticking my feet in the shoe-fitting fluoroscope X-ray machine. For a little kid, it was an imposing piece of equipment, encased in a walnut cabinet. You would step up onto a pedestal, stick your feet into a hollowed-out space, and then look through a screen to view the bones and soft tissue of your foot. Like countless other American children, I found this endlessly fascinating, and could spend all afternoon wiggling my toes in that machine. In later years, a historian wrote that fluoroscopes proved "as attractive and exciting to little customers as free balloons and all-day suckers," and they were a terrific help in fitting shoes. But by the early 1950s, fears of potential exposure to radiation gave the machines a bad reputation, and by the early 1960s, they were gone.

When I was nine years old, I began working at the store on Saturdays and in the summer. I was too young to do anything as intricate as sizing up the shoes and putting them in the right order, but they did find things for me to do.

Fred Krantz, who ran the stockroom back then, told me to sweep the floors. Even at that young age, I knew I had better work hard because I was the boss's son, and if I didn't do this job better than anyone else, people would make fun of me. Fred handed me a broom and a pail full of oiled sawdust, which I poured on the stockroom floor. After an hour of sweeping, the floor looked pretty good to me, so I told Fred I was done and asked for my next assignment.

"Let me take a look at it," he said. He examined the floor and then, without uttering another word, took the pail of sawdust and sprinkled it on the floor all over again. It wasn't good enough. I swept the floor again, until I completed the job to Fred's satisfaction.

During the Second World War, when there was a tremendous paper shortage, one of my jobs was to take the empty boxes, break down the four corners, flatten them out, pile them up, and then tie a string around them for recycling. As a young boy, I wasn't very strong, so breaking those boxes was hard work. But doing that job enabled me to earn my first money working for Nordstrom, and I remember the first time I stood in line to get my pay envelope (they paid in cash back then) along with all the other employees. I had made just a few dollars, but I was so proud.

A couple of days later, I overheard two of the office gals say, "Did you see Bruce standing in line for his pay envelope? Wasn't that cute? Mr. Everett came in just before Bruce and took the money out of his pocket and put it in the envelope. He said, 'Don't pay him out of the company payroll. He's not worth 25 cents an hour.'"

I was crushed. All these years later, I still haven't gotten over it.

Before World War II, Nordstrom was still a relatively small business. To help the company grow, Everett, Elmer, and Lloyd tried hard to develop good relationships with our shoe vendors, and as a result, they were liked and respected, which was very unusual in the industry.

I fondly recall the countless times when my dad brought home traveling salesmen and manufacturer's representatives for dinner and drinks. (If we'd had a larger house, we probably would have let them sleep there.) We got to know these salesmen well. Anne and I looked forward to one particular salesman coming to our house because he always brought us big all-day lollipops.

The store at Fifth and Pike, 1938

Customers wait outside the downtown Seattle store to
use their shoe ration stamps, circa 1942.

When I think back on those days, I wonder how my dad pulled this off because he was less outgoing than I am. Nevertheless, he was bound and determined to nurture relationships with those people, who appreciated our hospitality and became some of his best friends.

Those relationships came in handy during the Second World War, when merchandise was scarce. Because the leather supply and domestic footwear production were earmarked predominantly for military use, retailers were allowed only a limited quantity of shoes to sell. Once they started to run out of stock, many of our competitors chose to close up shop, even in the middle of the day.

The brothers did the opposite. I vividly remember the specific days during the course of the year when ration stamps came due and customers were allowed to use them to buy a pair of shoes. There were so many people lined up, waiting to get into our store, that the fire department would allow in only a certain number of people at one time. The customers would literally buy everything we had. Never has business been so easy. When people think they can't buy something, they want it even more — whether they need it or not. Because the brothers prepaid their suppliers, they were able to get deliveries when their competitors couldn't, so Nordstrom began to develop a reputation for being the store that had the shoes.

By the end of the war, we were well on our way to becoming the largest shoe store in America. For a town the size of Seattle, that was pretty good.

By the end of the war, we were well on our way to becoming the largest shoe store in America.

CHAPTER 2

MY PARENTS

Like most people, I am a combination of my mother and my father. My father taught and led by example, and I admired him in more ways than I can tell you. I wish I could be more like him. (I would hope that most sons would want to say that about their fathers.) While my mother was warm and gregarious, my dad was a quiet Swede, with an arm's-length personality. I'm a little more garrulous than he was. He wasn't afraid to take my pants down and whack me on the butt on occasion, but he was never mean. Although I didn't see much evidence of it, his close friends (who nicknamed him Whitey) thought he had a great sense of humor.

We didn't hug and kiss, but we did play catch every single night. When I saw the movie *Field of Dreams*, it moved me to tears because that was my dad and me. And like the lead character in that movie, I would give anything to have another chance to play catch with my dad.

Most people wouldn't think of Everett Nordstrom as a poker player, but he was a good one. I can remember one time, when I was in my thirties, playing in a poker game at the Seattle Golf Club. I had played poker all through college and thought I was pretty good. All of a sudden the door opened, and it was my dad. I was thinking, "I better shape up here." He asked if he could sit in on the game. Well, he beat me — and everybody else at the table — like a drum.

He had a poker face. But as the years went by, I knew him so well that I could detect his mood through the slightest change of expression.

My father was committed to (1) my mother, (2) his brothers, and (3) the whole Nordstrom family. He lived his life that way, and he set an example for me and my sister to do the same.

I don't think any wife loved her husband more

than my mother loved my dad.

My parents, Libby and Everett Nordstrom

My mother was named Elizabeth, but everyone called her Libby. She was a Southern girl who was full of life. Her family was from Texas, by way of Tennessee. After my maternal grandfather lost everything in the Depression, he moved his family to Seattle at the end of the 1930s. My mother went to the UW, as did my dad, and was also an accomplished singer who performed on the radio. (My dad couldn't carry a tune in a bucket.) She loved dancing and going out, and she and my dad, who was a tall, good-looking guy, made quite a pair.

She was a neat mom, the kind who made sure that our house was so inviting and comfortable that all the kids wanted to come over after school — just the way Fran, my late wife, did for our kids when they were little.

My mom, who taught me the social graces, was a big supporter of mine, and my personality is more like hers, while my sister's is more like our dad's. I always tell Anne that my dad loved her most, and she says my mother loved me most.

My dad was extremely proud of Anne, who was the smarter and more accomplished of the two of us for the first 20 years of our lives. I could make the case that she's still smarter. Anne is reserved, conservative, and driven. If she had been born 30 years later, she would be running this company for sure. She absolutely could do anything I could do in this business, but I'm not sure it would be as interesting to her as it is to me. As far as possessing the ability to assimilate the knowledge of this business and executing strategy, she would have been terrific. But she didn't want to make this a career. She wanted to be a mom, and is a very good one. She raised two terrific children, John and Susan, and also has a wonderful stepdaughter, Marnie Gittinger, with her husband, Wayne Gittinger.

I don't think any wife loved her husband more than my mother loved my dad. He always kissed her after dinner. Following his example, I've tried to show affection like that to both of my wives as a way of saying thanks.

I'll never forget something that was told to me by Lloyd's wife, my aunt Illsley, God bless her. When I was a young guy in the business, she took me aside and said, "Do you know what's wrong with you Nordstrom men? You never thank anybody and you never recognize people." I think she was talking about how we conducted our personal lives, with our wives and children. Guilty as charged, I think. It would be up to my mom to tell me that my dad was proud of me because it wasn't in his makeup to tell me directly. That's something I've tried to work on my whole life. I don't lavish praise on my sons, but I do praise them when they deserve it.

My mom was absolutely star-struck by my dad, who was her whole life until the day he died, in 1972. While she lived 14 more years after he passed away, her life was never the same.

Although she was not in the business, my mom occasionally had the opportunity to show off her creative side. When we started a line of private-label shoes, my dad asked her for some ideas for names, and she came up with Tony Garmo, Roberta, and many others.

My mother, who smoked like a chimney, eventually died of emphysema. Seeing her have to breathe through a machine for the last couple years of her life was scary, and it had a profound impact on me. But before that, I smoked cigarettes from age 17 to age 30. My dad often told me that I shouldn't smoke, and kept reminding me how bad it was for me. We had one of our few significant disagreements on that subject, and then he never mentioned it again.

Here's how I stopped smoking: In 1963, when I was coming back to work in the Seattle store after being in our Portland store, we threw a dinner party for my cousin John, who was going to take my spot in Portland. The party was at Bush Garden, the Japanese restaurant, and all our friends from Portland came to meet John and his wife, Sally. We were having a great time. I was smoking a cigarette, and John, who was sitting next to me, said, "You ought to quit smoking."

I said, "I can quit anytime I want."

He replied, "No, you can't."

"Yes, I can."

By this time, everybody was listening to this conversation and watching us. John took out his checkbook and, with a flourish, wrote me a check for a hundred dollars (which was a lot of money back then), and said, "Here's a hundred dollars. You can cash it. It's yours. But if you smoke one cigarette in the next year, you've got to give me two hundred dollars."

I got so mad. He really challenged me in front of all our friends. Finally, I took the check and started folding it and folding it. I tore it up into tiny little pieces and said, "I won't take your money. But I quit. I'll never smoke again."

And I never had another cigarette. Thank goodness John did that for me. I'll never forget when one of my heroes — Fred Hutchinson, the great baseball player and manager from Seattle — died of lung cancer. Wow! If it could happen to him, it could sure happen to me.

There were times when my dad talked to me and knew I wasn't paying attention, but he wasn't the kind of guy who would just hammer things into you. He would say, "Here's what I believe; accept it or not." As the years went by, I accepted it 99 percent of the time. He was right 100 percent of the time.

Anne, my dad, and me

ANNE GITTINGER

Anne held several positions in the company before starting a family. After her children were grown, we convinced her to return and head up the company's charitable contributions.

When I was younger, I worked in many different parts of the company. I stuffed account statements into envelopes, worked as an elevator operator and on the switchboard (which was the most fun), took credit applications, worked in the cash room, and was secretary to the treasurer of the company, Allan Goesling. For a few years, when we had the downtown, University, Portland, and Northgate stores (and before I became Allan's secretary), I did all the billing in the company. I handled every ledger, every charge, and every payment, and walked the trays back and forth. It was a very hands-on job. In today's computerized world, people laugh at the simplicity of the business in those days.

I remember Daddy showing me the room where they had installed the new computers that did the jobs that I had been doing manually for so many years. The room was climatized to keep the dust out. Daddy was shaking his head in amazement, and said, "Can you possibly believe this?"

I was dedicated to being a wife and mother and never thought about coming back to work full-time. But as the company was getting bigger and was receiving so many requests for contributions, it was clear that one person had to be responsible. By that time, my kids were in college and I was divorced. My brother said, "I have a job for you." An hour a week, he said. It obviously turned into something much bigger.

For 29 years I've been Director of Corporate Contributions, which has been wonderful. I love being here. I get to see my brother and the boys, and got to see my cousins John and Jim when they were here. I value the years I worked when Jim was here. John and I were very close in high school, and to this day are still very close.

*My grandfather (seated), my uncles, and my dad review the plans
for Northgate Mall with Northgate Development Management's
Jim Douglas (on right), around 1950.*

I give my father and uncles credit for having
the foresight and courage to
make the move to Northgate.

CHAPTER 3

LEARNING THE BUSINESS

When I was growing up, there were no shopping malls in the outlying areas. The only place to shop was downtown Seattle, which was a pretty hectic place. Believe it or not, we had bigger traffic jams then than we have now. In those days, there were streetcars on rails, and the traffic on all the streets ran both ways, unlike today, when most of the streets are one-way. Every morning, city crews cleaned the streets with water hoses that emerged from the sides of big tank-trucks.

In some ways, we were a small town out in the sticks, with all the insecurities of a small town. I've always been a sports wacko, who lived and died with the fortunes of our minor-league baseball team, the Rainiers, who were usually pretty good, but still minor league.

Because we had no major-league teams, we all closely followed the teams at the University of Washington, and whenever the Huskies won a game, it was a marvelous thing for all of us stuck way up here in the upper-left-hand corner of the country. Rowing has long been a popular sport around here, and when the eight-man rowing crew from the UW won the gold medal at the Olympic Games in 1936 in Berlin — Seattle's first international sports notoriety — that accomplishment satisfied us for about 15 to 20 years as our one claim to fame. My cousins John and Jim and I all rowed in college. John was a terrific oarsman who rowed in the UW's number one boat, which won the Henley Royal Regatta in England. Jim rowed on the freshman team, and I rowed on the lightweight-eight crew, for guys under 160 pounds.

The Smith Tower, at 42 floors, was the tallest building west of the Rockies, which made us feel that perhaps we weren't such a bush-league place after all. For 55 years, from 1914 to 1969, it was Seattle's tallest building, before it was dwarfed by the 50-story Seafirst Building. As I get older and look at the skyline of Seattle, I often reflect on the changes that have occurred in my hometown within my lifetime. I still think the Smith Tower is one of the prettiest buildings in the city.

The Boeing Company made Seattle important. In the Second World War, Boeing built the B-17s and other planes that helped win the war. All of a sudden, this little company in this little town was the preeminent builder of airplanes in the world.

During the war, Seattle became a point of debarkation for the troops, so a lot of people came through this town, and a lot of them stayed. Of course, they all needed shoes, and we Nordstroms were more than happy to take care of them.

Back in those days, our economy was fueled by fishing, logging, and airplanes. Today, we find ourselves led by Microsoft, Starbucks, Costco, Amazon.com, and, some might say, Nordstrom. How times have changed.

I continued to work at the store on Saturdays and during summer vacations. When I was about 12 or 13 years old, I started to notice girls, particularly the girls who worked as elevator operators in the store. (They were some of the few females working at Nordstrom, where probably 95 percent of the sales staff were men. Of course, the shoe business was male-dominated in those days.) We had one of the first automatic elevators, but customers didn't want to go up by themselves, so we had an elevator operator. My sister, Anne, did that job for a time. We had some interesting people who ran those elevators. The most famous was a West Seattle girl named Diane Friesen, who later changed her name to Dyan Cannon, became a noted movie actress, and married Cary Grant.

I started selling shoes when I was 14, in the bargain basement of our store. The manager was Cop Griffith, who was a great guy, but I don't think he was real pleased to have me imposed on him. He told me, "You're only going to sell slippers and tennis shoes because I don't want you to cripple anybody." That was frustrating because I wanted to compete with the people on the floor and run a big book of business. How could I do that when I was confined to selling items that cost only $2 or $3 a pair?

I would be working in the stockroom and somebody would say, "Bruce, could you get a pair of slippers for this lady?" Usually, they called me in desperation because there was nobody else available. After a month or so, they saw that I was okay, and I started getting calls, in order, like every other salesman.

*Boeing's new B-17 brought much excitement
to Seattle during the World War II years.*

Although I tried hard, I never was a very good salesman. I was plagued by my redheaded personality and my redheaded complexion, and I would often get just red-faced, embarrassed to tears. It was not easy for me to sit down in front of customers, engage them in a conversation, find out what they wanted, go to the back room to get the shoes, and then sell them to the customers. One of the reasons I tried hard to become a manager was the realization that I couldn't sell shoes for the rest of my life. That would kill me!

I think my grandpa sensed my difficulties. Back then, the sales floor was separated from the stockroom by curtains of Naugahyde strips, which you brushed aside to go in and out of the stockroom. I keenly — and fondly — remember sitting on a stool, helping a customer put on shoes, and then noticing out of the corner of my eye that those Naugahyde strips were parting, and then seeing this little face with glasses peering out from behind the curtain. It was my grandpa watching me sell. He did the same thing to my cousin John.

When people ask me if I felt I had to work in the family business, I say I never felt that. I was never encouraged or discouraged to work here by my dad, who used to say to me, "I don't care if you work around here. I just want you to work. Don't sit around and do nothing."

Some people who didn't know my dad assume that he held my hand as I learned the business. Not true. He rarely said much to me about what kind of job I was doing. He might make a gentle suggestion, but essentially his attitude was "It's your deal. You're going to sink or swim on your own." And that's the kind of manager I became. If I'm turning the decision-making over to you, the decisions — good or bad — are going to be yours, and the results — good or bad — are going to be yours. I'll take neither the glory nor the blame.

As I was progressing through my teenage years (which are difficult years for most everybody), whenever I would come to the store, I felt a level of confidence that I didn't have in any other aspect of my life. I knew that this business was the lifeline to my adulthood, and I knew that I could do the job because I had knowledge and experience. I never really thought about doing anything other than working in the store. The only other things I ever did outside the store were working in a fish cannery one summer in Alaska and serving in the Army when I got out of school.

I certainly knew the downside: The job of selling shoes requires lots of hours. It's sweaty and dirty. You're going back and forth to the stockroom all day, and you're down on your hands and knees waiting on customers, which I find an appropriate position for our level of service.

Back in those days, you had to wear a suit; no sport coat and slacks. For a time, the first and only suit I had was made of corduroy, and I wore it winter and summer. We didn't have air conditioning in those days, and when I wore that corduroy suit in the summer, it was so full of perspiration that you could wring it out like a washcloth at the end of the day.

To this day, I tell our people that I have done nearly everything within this company that I am asking them to do (as have my cousins and my sons), and that I thoroughly understand the things about our business that aren't pleasant. I don't know how you can run a business without that firsthand experience. Because my sons have sold shoes (or as we call it, "dogged" shoes), swept floors, and served as assistant managers, managers, and buyers, they come to their jobs with a knowledge of and respect for what it takes to succeed.

One of the bedrocks of our business is that there is only one path to the top and it begins on the sales floor, especially if your last name is Nordstrom.

There is only one path to the top and it begins on the sales floor, especially if your last name is Nordstrom.

SHOE VENDORS

Back in the 1940s and 1950s, our competition in Seattle was the department stores, Frederick & Nelson and The Bon Marché, as well as many specialty stores, including Leeds, Chandler's, and Bakers, which were all owned by Edison Brothers.

For many years, we didn't have any high-priced, high-fashion designer shoes. Instead, we carried basic, conservative, better lines of women's shoes from a vendor mix that included Selby Arch Preservers, Dr. Locke, Hill & Dale, and British Walkers. There was only one shade of brown, called Town Brown. Today, I don't know how many shades of brown we have.

There was a school of thought that big old Nordstrom shoe store couldn't sell high-priced shoes. Our first high-priced line was Julianelli, at $32.95. When I was selling, I didn't have the guts to bring a pair of those out to a customer.

In Portland, we later added Herbert Levine shoes, which in the 1950s and 1960s were worn by lots of movie actresses, as well as first ladies Jacqueline Kennedy and Pat Nixon. Although we didn't initially sell a lot of Herbert Levine shoes, we found that carrying them really made a difference in our business. When I became the buyer, we added Charles Jourdan, our first French-designer shoe, which retailed for $36.95 to $42.95. At the time I thought, "This is it. We've reached the top." Today, we have shoes that are $500 to $1,000, and we sell a lot of them.

In the 1960s and 1970s, we really jumped into young women's shoes, such as Joyce and Town & Country, and we became the place for teenagers to shop. Back-to-school business was fabulous. All of a sudden, my father and uncles started to realize that kids were great at bringing their parents to the store, and that if you took care of those kids, you could retain their business as they got older. From that time forward, that's been a very significant part of our thinking about shoes.

In men's shoes, we had all the right brands, and the two best sellers were both made by Winthrop; one had a capped toe and one had a plain toe. If you didn't have one of those two styles, you were not "with it."

THE DAWN OF SHOPPING CENTERS

In 1950, Seattle became a more cosmopolitan city with the construction of Northgate, which is considered one of the first shopping malls in the country. Right here in Seattle, Washington. That sounded like a pretty big deal to me.

Before Northgate was built, my dad and I drove out to the site. I was in high school at the time. The Interstate 5 freeway had not been built yet, so it took a while to get there. It was one big cow pasture. My dad said, "This is where we're going to build a store." I knew he was old (around 47), and I thought he had lost his marbles. I thought that building a store in the middle of nowhere was the dumbest thing I ever heard of.

But, of course, it wasn't so dumb after all. I give my father and uncles credit for having the foresight and courage to make the move to Northgate. Allied Stores, Inc., the developers of Northgate, had a tough time attracting tenants, so we were able to get the number one location, where we still are today. Back then we had a 5,000-square-foot shoe store; today it's a 122,000-square-foot full-line store.

Northgate was an immediate success, and it became a trendsetter. That success, of course, got people excited about building shopping centers outside city centers, a revolution that almost killed downtown retail in many places. Street retail gives human scale to a city. Without retail traffic, cities are left with nothing but office towers and become ghost towns after five o'clock.

LEASED SHOE DEPARTMENTS

Always looking for ways to expand their business, my dad and uncles began to take over leased shoe operations in department stores in the mid-1940s. Our first leased department was at Rhodes Department Store on First Avenue in Seattle, where I worked for a couple of years. The name Bruce Nordstrom didn't mean as much at Rhodes as it did at Nordstrom, so I was a little bit more on my own.

In order to get the right-size shoe from inventory, I often went back and forth between our store and Rhodes, which was four blocks away. I'd wait on my customer at Rhodes, get her size, then run as fast as I could to our Nordstrom store, where we had more inventory, then run back to my waiting customer at Rhodes. The customer would say to me, "Gee, I was worried you had died." I'd say, "I was just up in the stockroom." She didn't know that the stockroom was four blocks away.

Next, we leased the shoe departments at Olds & King in Portland, which was a part of Western Department Stores. Eventually, we leased departments all up and down the West Coast, and later throughout the West, in Tacoma, Oakland, Fresno, Sacramento, Albuquerque, Phoenix, San Antonio, and Honolulu.

With leased departments, we owned the inventory and furniture. The labels and shopping sacks had the name of the department store, but it was all our stuff. We hired and managed all the salespeople, but we had to abide by the stores' rules. We paid the stores a percentage of our volume, with a guarantee, and a percentage override. We had by far the biggest departments in these stores, and they represented pretty good cash-flow business for us. They helped our financial picture and enabled us to be more flexible.

On the other hand, we were invariably located in the third-rated department store in every town we were in. The leased operations didn't do much for our image and reputation, never gave us the feeling that they were getting us where we wanted to be, and were obviously not the future of our business. So when those stores started to have problems, we got out of them, thank goodness.

JOHN NORDSTROM

Like all of us, John started his career in the stockroom as a young boy. Later, when we entered the apparel business, John was responsible for starting our successful men's business, which he supported for many years. He was also responsible for men's shoes and operations.

I started working for the company when I was 13, as a stock boy at the University District store. My dad said I was worth about 15 cents an hour, and my check for two weeks' work was $5 or $6, with taxes taken out. A couple of years later, I started selling shoes in the children's shoe department downtown, where I learned the routine of stocking and selling all day.

I'm not sure that at the time, I ever thought this would be my career. I was interested mostly in boats, and when I was 16 or 17, I spent the summer working in a marina down on Lake Union, pumping oil and doing all sorts of jobs. That experience was a wake-up call because the manager was an alcoholic. I had never been around an alcoholic before, and I didn't understand the mood swings and the inconsistencies in behavior. After that, I thought this shoe business wasn't too bad after all.

In 1953, when I was a senior in high school, I sold men's shoes downtown. I liked that job because you made a little bit more money because the prices were higher, and men didn't fuss over their shoes the way women did. I was wet behind the ears, but I learned a lot by working with a group of older, professional shoe dogs who had been there a long time, and who were very friendly to me.

Those salesmen were completely different from the people who work for our company today. Back then, those guys were just working for the paycheck and were happy to come to work and sell shoes, with no aspiration to be managers. Our people today are more professional, and interested in achieving high goals.

I was the first manager of our Yakima shoe store, which consisted of a crew of five — four employees and me. For two years, I bought and managed men's, women's, and children's shoes, handbags, and hosiery, and did the windows and the janitorial work. We were very profitable because we kept our expenses down. They paid me $600 a month; my wife and I paid $200 for an apartment in Yakima. We eventually tore down that store and built a new one, which was twice the size of the original store. That experience was a big help to me in later years, as we began constructing stores all over the country.

MONKEY STORY

My dad was the merchandiser for children's shoes. He thought that having monkeys in the children's shoe department would be a big draw. Our Bellevue store had a big glass air-conditioned cage. In 1960, when we doubled the size of our Yakima store, we decided to build a similar cage there.

Far in advance of the store opening in Yakima, I arranged to buy two female monkeys. (I didn't think it would be a good idea to have a male and a female.) But a day before the opening, I was told that the monkeys would not arrive on time. I called up my brother, Jim, who was working with Jack McMillan in the Bellevue store, and asked him to bring his monkeys to Yakima for the opening.

After the store closed, Jim and Jack opened up the cage to get the monkeys, who were old and tough, and the monkeys got loose. Jack and Jim chased them for a couple of hours, until the monkeys ended up in a space in the false ceiling. They called the janitor, who was trusted by the monkeys because he fed them every day. He came to the store and was able to coax the monkeys into a perforated box for the trip to Yakima.

The only way they could fit the box into Jack's Ford Falcon mini station wagon was to put the tailgate down. Jack and Jim picked up Loyal and Sally and then left for Yakima. It was February, and by the time they got to Snoqualmie Pass, it had begun to snow, so they had to stop and put chains on their tires. (They were wearing their business suits at the time.) In order to do that, they had to put the box of monkeys on the ground. It was 25 degrees, and they were afraid the monkeys were going to freeze to death; Loyal and Sally were freezing in the car. Finally, they pulled up to the Yakima store at six in the morning. Right behind them was a Railway Express truck with the two monkeys I had ordered.

Left to right: Elmer, Everett, and Lloyd Nordstrom

They set a great example
for the guys of my generation.

CHAPTER 4

EVERETT, ELMER, AND LLOYD: THE WINNING TEAM

As I got older, I watched how closely my father and his brothers — who had 100 percent respect for each other — worked together, and it was fascinating to observe how they would defer to each other on their respective specialties. I've learned that if you're going to run a business by committee, that's absolutely necessary.

I have never known anybody smarter than my dad, who had a unique ability to get to the heart of the matter. The values of honesty and hard work, which he shared with his younger brothers, continue to this day to be the bedrock of our company. We couldn't do what we do if we didn't have those values, which manifest themselves in many different ways. Every day in every store in every region, we hope that something positive is happening that will reinforce our reputation and make things better for our employees.

Dad believed strongly in the things that make our company unique and solid: Give the customer a good value, treat people fairly, allow all employees to contribute their thoughts and make their own mistakes, and finally, set a goal and devote yourself to its completion. As he always said, winning and success are fun and profitable, so why not devote that little extra effort?

My dad was a big believer in employees using a calendar pad for recording all the things they needed to do each day, and training themselves to do the most important things first. Generally, number 8 on your list is more fun than number 1, but you'd better first take care of number 1, even if it's painful.

He was the bottom-line guy — the best businessman and the best retailer that I've ever known. Period. He was very good with numbers and paid careful attention to expenses and expense-savings and running a trim ship. He was also intensely focused on increasing sales. To do that, you have to have a feel for all phases of the business: fashion, people, display, receiving, and marking.

Everett Nordstrom

He took a course on real estate at the UW, covering, among other things, business rents. By applying what he learned to some of the first leases our company negotiated, we were able to get excellent terms and interesting provisions. Let's say we projected that a new Nordstrom would generate $1 million a year. My dad would tell the developer that we would pay 4 percent rent on the first million, but if we reached a million and a half, we'd pay 3 percent rent, and so on; the percentage would go down as the volume went up. The developer thought we would never reach our projections, but we always did. As we got up into the big numbers, our average rent kept going down, and for some stores, we got the percentage down to next to nothing. Creating a carrot for ourselves to generate great business was a real selling point to these developers. To the best of my knowledge, no other retailer back then came up with that kind of lease arrangement.

Nowadays, it almost works the opposite. The opening costs don't sink you as much. Because you want to have a profit as quickly as you can, you can't carry an exorbitant occupancy cost. I look back, and I still think the original way should be the way to go.

Anybody who knew Uncle Elmer would smile when they thought of him because he had this wonderfully twinkly dry sense of humor. With Elmer, as with my dad, you had to prove yourself; you had to accomplish something before he'd compliment you (which is probably the way it should be). My dad oversaw finance, while Elmer was the number one guy for backroom operations — shipping, marking, receiving, janitorial, and so on. He also oversaw men's and children's footwear and dealt with the sales clerks' union.

Like his brothers, Elmer loved sports. But he had health problems growing up, so he devoted much of his time to his boats and to all things mechanical; he was the most mechanically adept of the brothers.

Elmer devoted much of his civic life to Seattle's Swedish Hospital, which was founded in 1910 by his future father-in-law, Dr. Nils A. Johanson, a prominent surgeon. Dr. Johanson was not too thrilled about his daughter, Kitty, marrying a shoe salesman. Nevertheless, in 1934, shortly after Elmer and Kitty married, Elmer was placed on the board of Swedish as a non-salaried volunteer. I've always felt that one of the reasons Elmer worked so hard for the success of Swedish Hospital was that he wanted to show his father-in-law that Kitty had picked the right guy. Today, Swedish Medical Center is considered the best hospital in our region, and one of its crown jewels is the Elmer J. Nordstrom Medical Tower, which was made possible through contributions from the Nordstrom family.

Lloyd, who joined the business in 1933 after college graduation, was the director of advertising and public relations, and shared with Everett the buying and merchandising of women's shoes, which represented the bulk of the business for many years. Lloyd was the most natural merchant and probably the best salesman of the three brothers, and he

Lloyd Nordstrom

had a feel for fashion comparable to that of my son Pete today. Lloyd, the tallest and handsomest of the brothers, brought savoir faire to the party. He and his wife, Illsley, lived a little fancier lifestyle than Everett and Elmer and their families, but he had the same work ethic and drive to make our company succeed. He served honorably as an officer in the U.S. Navy in the Second World War. He was a wonderful man.

Everett and Lloyd played lots of sports. Lloyd was an excellent athlete, the best of the three. As an undergraduate at the UW (where he was also class president), he was the starting center on the Husky basketball team. From 1930 through 1932, Lloyd was a nationally ranked intercollegiate tennis player, and was also the Washington State singles champion and Pacific Coast doubles champion. When he played at Forest Hills, New York (where the U.S. Open was held), he competed in singles and doubles against the great players of the day.

In 1989, Lloyd's family donated $2.5 million to the university to build the Lloyd Nordstrom Tennis Center, one of the Northwest's most modern indoor tennis facilities, located just north of Husky Stadium. The tennis center, which has six courts, has helped the Huskies recruit top players who ordinarily might not want to come to a place where it has been known to get cold and rainy on occasion.

Lloyd told me many times that everything he learned about sports he learned from my dad. When my dad was in high school, he was captain of the football, basketball, and baseball teams for the "midgets" (as they were called in those politically incorrect days) — a separate division for players under 120 pounds.

When they left the store, the three brothers generally went their separate ways and didn't do a lot of interacting socially. If two of them got together, it would usually be Lloyd and my dad, who played golf together. Elmer preferred boating or tinkering with cars, which he loved.

My cousins and I admired how they handled family situations — wives and children. The classic example was summer vacations. Seattle summers are short. If one brother had two weeks off around the Fourth of July, one of the other brothers' wives might say, "How come we don't get those two weeks off?" Boy, they would cut that conversation right off and it wasn't brought up again. That was when I first became aware that the brothers' wives didn't get along 100 percent of the time. Everett, Elmer, and Lloyd had agreed that anything that had to do with the business was not going to be the subject of a debate within the family, and didn't want any pettiness to creep into business decisions. On Saturdays during college football season, they would flip a coin to see who would go to the Husky game because one of them had to be minding the store. They set a great example for the guys of my generation.

Everett and Elmer with their proud dad, 1949

I am second from the left in this Beta Theta Pi fraternity photo, 1951.

I learned a lot about
human relationships
from the fraternity.

CHAPTER 5

UNIVERSITY OF WASHINGTON

When I enrolled at the University of Washington, I continued to work at the stores on the weekends, some afternoons, the Half-Yearly Sales, and all summer. Because I worked on Saturday, I tried to get to sleep early on Friday night, which was not easy when you lived in a fraternity house. I remember sleeping on a sleeping porch in the Beta Theta Pi fraternity house, when everybody else was rolling in at three a.m., rousting me out of bed. Those were hard Saturdays when I had to get up early to go to work.

College was a wonderful experience for me. It allowed me to mature and grow up. I procrastinated in many of my studies and wasn't a great student, but my dad never got after me. He'd say, "It's your life. I think it's in your best interest to apply yourself a little bit more." I didn't apply myself until I started working, then I really applied myself. All he wanted me to do was work.

I lived in the Beta Theta Pi house all four years I attended the U. I loved the fraternity life and enjoyed myself as much as anyone. I was social chairman of my pledge class, and later vice president of the house and song leader. The rush chairman was Bud Erickson, who many years later became our director of store planning.

I learned a lot about human relationships from the fraternity, where I saw the value of getting to know people from different walks of life and economic strata. Living with guys from farms, big cities, and suburbs, I learned that not everybody is the same. Some guys you like better than others; some do more work within the fraternity than others. But if you work together as a group, you can really accomplish a lot.

That experience made me a big advocate of living groups, whether it's a church group, a dorm, or a fraternity house. If you're attending a school like the UW that has over 40,000 students (17,000 when I was there), it's too big to absorb and connect socially. It's important to make a connection, to have somebody to go to the movies with, to double date with, to even have a beer with on occasion. Those experiences help you grow up a little bit.

For some 20-odd years, our fraternity won the award for having the most lettermen on campus. Being a sports nut, I enjoyed associating with those guys and getting to know them. Most of them were terrific fellows, and you could see why they succeeded: they rolled up their sleeves and really worked hard. We've had people work for us in our stores who were good at sports but didn't do well here, and I would say to them, "If you had worked as hard on this business as you did lifting weights or running laps, you'd be a terrific success."

One of my closest friends from college is Wayne Gittinger, who played varsity baseball. Wayne is a native of Kellogg, Idaho, where he was a high-school star — captain of the football, basketball, and baseball teams. I remember going with him into a tavern in Kellogg and seeing his picture plastered all over the place. Kellogg is a silver-mining town, and both of Wayne's parents worked in the mines. His family home was right near the entrance to a mine.

Wayne and I used to work together at the Lake City Tavern, where he was the bartender and I was the server, carrying pitchers of beer to the tables. I think we pumped more beer than any other tavern in the state of Washington.

After a few years at the Seattle law firm Lane Powell, Wayne became our corporate counsel. Ever since he became a member of our board of directors, in 1971, Wayne has been an invaluable source of advice and counsel to this company. Although he retired from the board in 2005, he continues to be called on for his wisdom and guidance. Wayne, who is married to my sister, Anne, has a proprietary feeling about Nordstrom. Knowing Wayne as well as I do, I don't think the retail business is a natural part of his makeup, yet he loves it. I am not the only one in the Seattle business community who believes that Wayne, now a senior partner at Lane Powell, is the best attorney in town.

WAYNE GITTINGER

Wayne is the company's longtime corporate counsel, and has been a director since 1971, when we first went public. He married my sister, Anne, in 1984.

Bruce and I met in 1951, when we were in the same class at the University of Washington. We had many mutual friends, but we joined different fraternities; he was a Beta, I was an SAE (Sigma Alpha Epsilon), and my fraternity house was a block down the street from the Beta house.

While we were at the UW, a mutual friend of ours, Otto Geisert, was part owner of the Lake City Tavern, which was a college hangout. Otto got both of us jobs; I tended bar and Bruce was occasionally a waiter. I don't think he spilled any more beer than the rest of us.

I got out of the Coast Guard on August 29, 1959, and joined the law firm Lane Powell on August 30, 1959. Under the tutelage of my partner George Powell, I did quite a bit of work for Simpson Timber Company, and I worked closely with Simpson's president, Henry Bacon, who was a good friend of Everett, Elmer, and Lloyd Nordstrom.

In the 1960s, when Bruce, Jim, John, and Jack took over, their dads said they could hire their own accountants, lawyers, etc. I got a call one day from Bruce, who asked me to be their lawyer.

Bruce and I would often have coffee at a hamburger place on Fourth Avenue, across from where Littler's men's store used to be. I remember him coming in one day and saying, "This is a big day. We just got our sales figures for last year: $46 million." He was all smiles that day.

Bruce is genuine, loyal to friends and employees, full of energy, and interested in the problems and successes of others. Not a real good golfer, though.

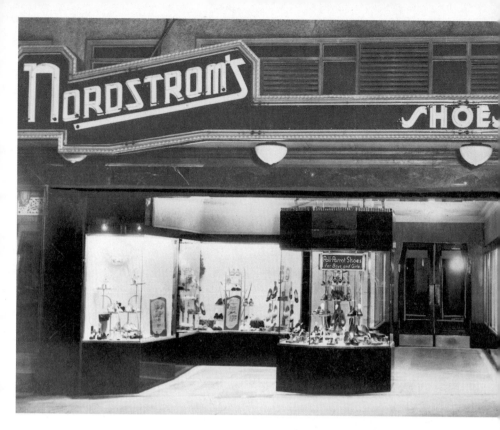

Our University District store in the 1930s

A small store is like a crucible; it gives you **hands-on experience** and an appreciation for what every job in the company entails.

CHAPTER 6

GETTING DOWN TO BUSINESS

I graduated from the UW in early 1956, but I am officially a member of the class of 1955. Shortly after graduation, I received my commission in the Army as a second lieutenant, and served for six months at Fort Bliss, in El Paso, Texas. (As an undergraduate, I was involved in the Reserve Officers' Training Corps.)

When I got back from Fort Bliss, I was asked to run our University District store, which was one of two branch stores at the time. The brothers had opened the store, on University Avenue between 45th and 46th Streets, in 1923. Opening that store — which carried men's, women's, and children's shoes, plus handbags and hosiery — was a good decision because The Ave. was a great place in those days, with a wonderful collegiate atmosphere that attracted lots of shoppers from nearby neighborhoods such as Laurelhurst, Windermere, and View Ridge. My dad and uncles all took turns managing that small store, which employed about a dozen people and generated about $250,000 to $300,000 a year in volume.

I enjoyed managing the store; I wasn't cowed by it and I felt that, even though I was just a kid, I knew enough to do it. I learned a lot because a small store is like a crucible; it gives you hands-on experience and an appreciation for what every job in the company entails. I bought the women's shoes, lugged the cartons into the stockroom, put the shoes out on display, trimmed the windows, swept the floors, took out the garbage, and was the HR person. (Of course, we didn't call it "HR" in those days.)

A lot of times I was there by myself and had to sell items such as hosiery, not an easy task for me. I'd get the Hanes hosiery boxes out and a female customer would say, "I'd like to see it on skin." I had seen our female employees stick their hands in the hosiery so the customer could see what it looked like on skin, but I've got this red complexion and red hair. I'd stick my hand in the hosiery and all this red hair started coming through. It was not a pleasant sight.

We hired a lot of good people who were working their way through school. It was a good job for an ambitious kid who needed the money.

Because it was commission, you could work really hard for a few hours and make quite a bit of money. Those were the kinds of people we were trying to appeal to — not people who were just interested in punching a clock and going through the motions. Many of them made Nordstrom their career, but we also employed a lot of people who eventually became prominent professionals in town.

This experience gave me a sense of self-respect because I ran that little store pretty well. We beat the previous year's numbers, which gave me a lot of personal satisfaction. It was probably the first time in my life that I was doing something that, to me, was meaningful. I won the respect of some of the old-timers who worked for us, including an old Norwegian named Elmer Tuleen, who rarely had any expression on his face. But things changed toward the end of my tenure in that store — I connected with him, and I think I connected with every other employee in the store as well.

Not that I didn't make my share of mistakes. In a "State of the Company" presentation that I gave to our employees in early 1971, I talked about the importance of never letting down our high standard of service. About that time, J. C. Penney, one of our pioneer retailers, had just passed away. When Mr. Penney was running his very first store in Wyoming in 1902, before closing the door for the night, he would go out onto the street and look both ways to make sure he wasn't shutting out a customer. In my presentation to our employees, I compared Mr. Penney's actions with the behavior of one of our own young executives: A few years back, while closing the doors for the night, he wouldn't let a customer in to make a phone call simply because it was after hours. I don't know if this fellow was just going by the rules or whether he was overly impressed with his own importance. The fact is that he showed very poor judgment. I hate to say it, but I was that young manager, and I have regretted that action all of these years and have earnestly tried to never unnecessarily offend a customer again.

IMPORTANCE OF SIZES

One of the characteristics of our business has been making sure we're in stock in a full range of sizes. To this day, I don't understand why retailers don't exploit wide and deep inventories to attract customers. Early on, my dad made mathematical studies of what sizes sold. He put percentages on each one of the sizes, not just on average sizes; he went all the way out to size 12 and 13 in women's shoes and 18 in men's, and all the widths. His point was that there are customers for those sizes. There aren't a lot of them, but if you get those customers, they tell all their friends.

When I was managing the University District store, my dad would often come in, and he'd go into the back and look at the inventory, the size range, and everything. One time, he commented that we were missing 7B (which was the average size at the time) in a popular shoe.

I said, "I know that. It's a hot shoe. We sold them all out."

He said, "You shouldn't be missing a size." We kind of got into it a little and growled at each other. I said, "I have it on order."

He said, "Let me see that order." I went back to the files and showed him my order slip. Sure enough, I had several 7Bs ordered, but that didn't satisfy my dad, who ceremoniously took one of the order slips, folded it up, stuck it on the shelf, and said, "The next time a customer comes in asking for a 7B, try that one on them."

As usual, he was right. A shoe style is hot because people want it, so we'd better have it in stock. Every business lesson my dad ever taught was built around the idea of taking care of every single customer, of treasuring every single customer. If you do that, you'll sell a lot of shoes.

Good ideas have come from all parts of this company. You have to create a culture where people feel secure about offering ideas.

Fred Rady, the first manager of our Portland store, established a wonderful tradition for improving our business. Every night after the store closed at six o'clock, all the employees sat together in a half-circle around Fred, who would go from salesperson to salesperson and ask one question: "What did you miss today?"

Every business lesson my dad ever taught was built around the idea of taking care of every single customer, of treasuring every single customer.

When I went to work in the Portland store, the manager was Ray Highbarger, who continued the tradition that Fred had started. The first time Ray asked me what I had missed that day, I felt like a dope because I hadn't thought about it. But from that day forward, I made sure that I wrote down what people asked for that we didn't have. That information helped me to spend my day more productively. Furthermore, I learned to be more sensitive to what was happening around me, to notice what was hot and what was not, to be aware of what worked and what didn't work. That's the level of awareness all of our entrepreneurial salespeople must have in order to run their own little business within Nordstrom.

When I started running our Portland stores, I continued to do what Fred and Ray had done. At weekly meetings, I would ask each salesperson: "What did you miss this week?" I remember that one salesman said, "I had a lady who wanted a navy blue pump, and we didn't have a size 7B." That's ridiculous. You can't run a shoe store without a 7B in a navy blue pump. The minute the meeting was over, I called Seattle and asked them to send us 20 separate styles in 7B pumps. They put the pumps on the Greyhound bus, and we had them on the floor that afternoon. This action helped give me credibility with the sales crew because I responded to what they asked for.

Today, with the information technology we have, we are able to move quickly to ensure that we are always in stock.

You have to create a culture where people feel secure about offering ideas.

NORDSTROM'S

half-yearly

shoe sale

As always, the Northwest's largest!
3 floors, 3 stores of famous-brand shoes!

Over 20,000 pairs of shoes for men, women and children are included in this great sale! There are more shoes, more styles, more sizes featured in this sale at savings, than most shoe stores ever have in their entire stocks! So come, find shoes to fit everyone in the family .. at welcome reductions.

Highlights of the Sale!

WOMEN'S FASHION SHOES
Regularly 14.95 to 32.95 NOW 10⁹⁰ to 19⁹⁰

WOMEN'S BUDGET FLOOR SHOES
Regularly 6.95 to 12.95   NOW 4⁹⁰ to 8⁹⁰

CHILDREN'S and BOYS' SHOES
Regularly 5.95 to 9.95 NOW 3⁹⁰ to 6⁹⁰

SECOND FLOOR CASUALS and Demi-Heels 7⁹⁰ to 14⁹⁰
Regularly 9.95 to 19.95   NOW

WOMEN'S SPECIALIZED FITTING DEPT. 11⁹⁰ to 15⁹⁰
Regularly 16.95 to 24.95 NOW

WOMEN'S
- JULIANELLI
- PALTER DE LISO
- PALIZZIO
- D'ANTONIO
- KIMEL
- DE LISO DEBS
- HILL & DALE
- NATURALIZERS
- MR. NEAL
- FIANCEES
- RISQUES
- SELBY
- DR. LOCKE
- FLORSHEIM
- JOYCE
- TOWN & COUNTRY
- AMALFI
- PENALJO
- BRITISH BREVITIS
- CAPEZIO

CHILDREN'S & BOYS'
- STRIDE RITES
- GERWINETTES
- GRO-TRU
- WINTHROP, JR.

MEN'S
- WRIGHT ARCH PRESERVER
- JOHNSTON & MURPHY
- NUNN-BUSH
- EDGERTON
- JOHN MARTIN
- WINTHROP

Shop Downtown Tonight 'til 9!

Nordstrom's

FIFTH AT PIKE • UNIVERSITY WAY • NORTHGATE
OPEN MON. EVE   OPEN THURS. EVE   OPEN WED., FRI. EVE
ALL NORDSTROM'S STORES OPEN MONDAY MORNING AT 9:30

*This newspaper ad is from about 1956, when I
was managing the University store.*

*Bob Weil and Adolph Frank, two managers who had what
it takes, attend a recognition dinner in the 1990s.*

Good managers
must be selfless.

CHAPTER 7

WHAT IT TAKES TO BE
A MANAGER

Although the pace of our business is faster today, the basic challenges remain the same: find the right employees, take care of the customers, and make a profit.

If we asked every person we were about to hire this question — "Are you ambitious?" — 100 percent of them would answer, "Yes, I am ambitious." Do you know how many are really ambitious? Maybe 2 percent. You sure can't discover the successful people just by interviewing them. I've hired people who were quiet but turned out to be great salespeople.

Waiting on a customer in a shoe department is not the easiest job in the world. It's hard work. Either you can do it or you can't. So, then, how do you find out if someone is really ambitious and can do the job? With us, it's "Here's your shoehorn; now go to work." Sink or swim. On-the-job training. Although we do provide some introductory training for new employees, particularly in learning the technical nuts-and-bolts part of our business, the real test is how they perform on the sales floor. In the first few months of employment, there is quite a turnover because a lot of people find out that this is not for them. But we have relatively lower turnover after people have been here a year or so.

Because we promote from within, we need to see whether a salesperson can make the transition to assistant manager. You must really want to do this because becoming an assistant manager usually means that your pay decreases. In our company, a good commission salesperson could make more than an assistant manager, who gets a salary but must also continue to sell.

There are a lot of top salespeople who don't necessarily make good managers. Not only do managers have to have good sales records, but they also have to do some obvious things such as coming to work on time. In the old days, a lot of stars didn't do that; they preferred to operate on their own schedule.

When I was younger and more directly connected with the floor, I was hiring and firing managers of departments and, in some cases, managers of stores. In the cases where it didn't work — where someone was either demoted or let go — I would meet with these people and discuss the reasons for my decision. The soon-to-be-former manager would say, "I don't get it. Last year, I was the hero around here, and now I'm gone."

My pitch back to them was that if you worked as hard today as you did to get to this management job, you'd still be having success. Sometimes when people become executives, they think they can just sit at their desk and not have to work as much; they think they don't have to get their hands dirty.

That's why good managers must be selfless. When we are evaluating managerial candidates, we want to know if they are the kind of people who proactively look for other things to do to help the company. Do they volunteer to work on the displays a couple of days a week? In the old days, the sales records of all the salespeople were kept on paper, and people would volunteer to help keep track of them, which would make reordering easier. Those voluntary actions make an impression, and tell you that a person is a candidate for advancement in this company.

Sometimes, you improve morale by parting company with somebody who you find out is a pain in the neck in the department.

I encourage our managers to keep on finding ways to crank it up a little bit. For example, I tell them, if you're on a plane flying to New York on a buying trip, read *Vogue* rather than *Sports Illustrated* because *Vogue* is going to help you do your job. Everything you do can be related back to our business.

One time, I needed a new main-floor women's shoe buyer, and I decided to go outside our company to hire a traveling shoe salesman who used to come in and take sizes for us. I thought I knew him very well. He was clean-cut, from a nice family, and he worked hard. I told him I would make an exception to our hiring policy and bring him in at the buyer level. Although he would not make as much money as he had been making before, the future looked good for all of us, and there would be many potential opportunities. I hired him and he was terrible. He couldn't make his figures. Worse, he had a secret drinking problem. That was the biggest swing and a miss I ever had.

You might think of salespeople as being gregarious. Not necessarily. They come in all shapes, colors, and personalities. What they have in common is that they are true to themselves. If you aren't true to yourself, customers will see right through you.

A good leader must cultivate mavericks who can succeed within the framework of the organization. (You must be careful because some mavericks are destructive to what you're trying to do.) Back in the 1970s, Caroline Howard was the buyer for our Brass Plum (juniors) department. She didn't look or sound the part, but she was terrific. Instead of going to Frederick & Nelson or The Bon Marché to see what was selling, Caroline would get ideas for our fashion direction by going out to the University District and exploring the small avant-garde shops, to see what was happening, and then develop items that were unique to our store. She did that over and over again. Whenever I would make a comment about her to my cousin Jim, who was her boss, he would say, "Listen, leave her alone." He was exactly right.

SOME TOP MANAGERS

In our formative years, we were fortunate to have many great managers, such as Tex Hartley. Tex joined our company in 1954 and for more than two decades ran our leased shoe departments throughout the West, helping to make it a very profitable business. Tex, who had tremendous drive and zeal to succeed, was great on expenses and understood the

Tex Hartley

basic middle-price customer, which was the target customer for those departments. He was one of the first winners of the John W. Nordstrom Award, which is the highest accolade you can earn in our company. Tex loved my dad, and my dad loved him; he thought of my dad as a second father.

One time, I received a letter from the president of Rhodes Department Store in reference to building plans for their store in Albuquerque, where we were leasing a shoe department. He asked me to fire Tex because, he said, Tex had overstepped his bounds by asking the architect for the new store to make an opening in front of the shoe department; the original plans had it walled off. I wrote him back, saying, "Tex has operated our leased shoe departments for many years, through six presidents of Rhodes, and he will continue to do a great job." End of discussion.

Adolph Frank, who joined Nordstrom in 1950, was a wonderful salesman even though he was one of the quietest guys in our company. Natty, broad-shouldered, and muscular, Adolph started working in our store's budget basement around the same time I did, but unlike me, he was incredibly successful. How did he do it? I figured that I needed to learn his secret, so when he was taking care of a customer, I would sidle over to him to try to hear what he was saying. But he was so soft-spoken, I could never quite make out what he said. Next thing I knew, he was carrying a few pairs of shoes up to the desk and then wrapping them up for the customer.

For years, when Adolph was selling shoes on the main floor, I would run stock with him. I would sweat a lot, but he was always neat. I don't know how that happened.

Adolph was his own person. He just knew that he wanted to do well and make a lot of money. When he expressed interest in becoming a manager, we weren't sure he would make it, but he turned into a great manager for us at our stores in Alderwood and Aurora Village. When he was selling, he didn't have that proprietary feeling. But when he got management responsibility, it became his business. That's what you want.

Adolph worked for us as a buyer, department manager, and store manager for 36 years, including 10 years in Yakima, where he hired a teenage girl named Gail Cottle, who rose through our ranks to become an executive vice president. Long after he retired, we still called on Adolph to fill in as a manager when somebody took a vacation for a couple of weeks.

Sadly, Adolph passed away in 2006. I had never seen so many people at a funeral. The love expressed by his family and friends came as no surprise to any of us whose lives were touched by this special man.

When I began selling shoes for our company, one of our great stars was Harry Home, who had joined Nordstrom in 1946 at the ripe old age of 18. Harry, a native of Vancouver, British Columbia, began selling shoes when he was 13 years old.

Harry loved my dad and worshipped his leadership. When he was 22 years old, Dad made him buyer of main-floor ladies' shoes, our single biggest department. There is a famous story in our company about the time Dad took Harry to New York for his first trip as the buyer. They visited a sample room in New York, and everyone greeted my dad and began talking to him about their new line. Before they got going, my dad told them: "Don't talk to me, talk to my buyer, Harry Home." Then he turned around and left. Harry would later say, "There's not enough money in the world for me to pay Mr. Everett for what he did for me."

One time when I was a stockboy, I was bringing up a load of shoes from the basement, huffing and puffing, and Harry saw me and said, "You looked just like your dad when you did that." I think that was one of the best compliments I ever received.

Harry preceded me in a lot of positions, including main-floor ladies' shoe buyer in Seattle. I was getting promoted because Harry was getting promoted. He was successful as a manager because he wanted to be on the sales floor all the time, regardless of his position. He had wonderful communication skills, which are essential to being a good manager. I've seen too many managers who are smart, hardworking, clean, reverent, brave, and true, but then when they get in front of their troops — who want to be led and given ammunition to help them succeed — those managers can't do it in a way that's impactful.

I fondly recall the staff meetings that Harry would lead every Saturday morning. He'd bring out boxes of new shoes, open them one at a time, and say, "You guys aren't going to believe what I'm about to show you. I'm holding some of the best shoes that we've ever had in this store. You're going to see an array of color that we've never had before." That wasn't a phony deal; he thought that every shoe he bought was the best shoe ever. He described these shoes as "an acre of diamonds."

Harry would open the lid of each box, take out the tissue, and caress the shoe. It was like you were looking at a beautiful woman. It was fabulous. When the customers would come into the store, we would repeat what he had told us.

Today, we try to get our department managers to have that same kind of proprietary feeling, but that's hard to do because we're so much bigger. We can't have a buyer in every store, but we've got to come up with other ways to ensure that the people in every store feel that they are working in a special place and that they own "a piece of the rock." They need to know that their sweat and caring will carry the day.

By the way, when we consider managers for promotion, many times it comes down to which person has gone through a rough patch of business and has overcome that adversity. I've been around long enough to realize that you don't really know enough about people until you see how they react when things are not going their way.

My dad was perceptive about what people had in them, and he brought the best out of them. I give my dad and uncles the credit for throwing the ball to these young buyers and telling them to "go get 'em."

When I was a young person, we weren't open on Sunday and we were open only a couple of nights a week, depending on the location of the store. (I'm not so sure that we didn't work more hours back then than they do now.) I wanted to be there when the store was open, when people were coming through the door. I was always running a little scared, worried that maybe there was something going on that I should know about.

When I got out of the Army, my dad advised me to work every hour I could, work as hard as I could, think about the business 24 hours a day, and do it for five years. And then, he said, I'll discover that that's what I do. It will be something that is ingrained in me. Sure enough, I followed his advice, and it was ingrained in me.

You don't really know enough about people until you see how they react when things are not going their way.

Tex worked at Nordstrom from 1954 until 1982, and was a recipient of the John W. Nordstrom Award. For 24 years, he oversaw 17 leased departments (each with its own buyer), from San Francisco to San Antonio, and he was on the board of directors for nine years. Before he joined Nordstrom, Tex was working at a shoe store in Oakland, California. He asked a friend if he would introduce him to the Nordstroms when they next visited Oakland.

I met Lloyd and told him I wanted to be the buyer at the leased shoe department in Oakland. Lloyd told me that Nordstrom didn't give buying jobs to outside people; they promoted from within. After a couple of meetings, Lloyd said to me, "Tex, come over here as the assistant manager." I said, "I will do that, and if I do a good job, will you give me the first opening you have as a buyer?" He said, "Okay, done deal." Two months later, he transferred the buyer to Portland and made me the buyer of the Oakland store. Lloyd was a man of his word, and was faithful to the people who worked for the company.

What impressed me most about Nordstrom was that they gave everybody the freedom to succeed and the leeway to use our ideas and skills to the fullest. They never said no, and that is a fact. Never did I have any Nordstrom family member check on me or tell me how much money to spend.

When national shoe salesmen would come to Seattle to sell to us, Everett, Elmer, and Lloyd would stop by to personally thank them for coming to Seattle to give us a special showing. One time when I was working with vendors and had a lot of shoes on the floor of the showroom, Everett came over to me, sat down, and whispered in my ear: "Tex, are you going to buy all those shoes?" I said, "Yes, Mr. Everett, it's the hottest line I've got." He said: "Well, Tex, that's why we've got good buyers like you. You know what you're going to need." That was the way Everett built people up.

In 1946, a teenaged Harry Home joined Nordstrom as a shoe salesman and rose through the ranks, working in the downtown Seattle and University stores, the Portland store, and the leased departments at Rhodes and Lou Johnson. He became a buyer at 22, and noted, "I took Bruce on his first trip East."

When we started to grow, I remember Mr. Everett came to me and said, "We have a bit of a problem. With multiple stores, we Nordstroms are not going to be able to be there to watch them. We have to add a philosophy: Let's get concerned about one customer and one pair of shoes. If we do that, everything will fall into place." That was so astute. Mr. Everett was a giant of a man; he was the best retailer in America.

The desire to sell more stuff was ingrained in our makeup, and we did a good job of accomplishing that.

The Nordstrom family has passed on the principles of what they thought was right in running a business, and this has never changed through four generations. It's like esprit de corps in the Marine Corps (I served in the Marines). It develops through the people, not the commanding general.

We hired people with the desire to succeed, rather than people with knowledge about shoes or retail. If they really wanted to get ahead, we could help them get there. But first, we needed to see the spark in those people in order to make them into real customer-service people. To boost their self-esteem, I always sold the premise: You are not good because you are at Nordstrom, you are at Nordstrom because you are good.

ADOLPH FRANK

Adolph started on the Budget Floor at the Fifth and Pike store in 1950, at the age of 25, and stayed with the company until his retirement in 1986. In the years after his retirement, he was called upon several times to be an interim store manager.

From the day I began working at Nordstrom, I immediately felt at home. John W. Nordstrom set an example for all of us by coming to the store every day in a suit, walking around the store, and speaking to everybody. Mr. Everett did that as well. Bruce is a carbon copy of his dad, and Blake is a carbon copy of Bruce. They all make it a point to talk to everyone.

Mr. Everett, who taught me that a manager surrounds himself with good people, always said: "You are only as good as your people."

Everett would listen to you. He'd sit back in his chair, put his hands behind his head, and just listen, never interrupting you.

The first time I became a store manager, I had what I thought was a serious problem, so I called Everett for some advice. He said, "Whose store is it?" I didn't know whether to say "yours" or "mine." He said, "I could give you an answer. I could make a decision for you, but it would still be your fault if it was wrong. You make the decision."

From that, I learned that if I ever had a problem, I didn't need to call them. The Nordstroms always said, "It's your store. You run it the way you would if your name were on the building."

I told managers to not be afraid to make a mistake. If you've never made a mistake, you've never done anything. Just don't make the same mistake twice. For buyers, if you never made a mistake, you'd never have anything to put on sale.

When it came to selling shoes, these were our rules:

1. Measure both feet.

2. Bring out four pairs of shoes.

3. Stand when the customer is standing.

4. Walk to the mirror with the customer.

5. Let the customer sit in the chair and you bring over the shoes.

6. Always give the customer your card, whether you sold them or not.

Of the four pairs of shoes that I would bring out, one or two pairs would be what the customer asked for, and the other pairs were completely different. I tried not to confuse the customers. If they didn't like the shoes, I'd take them back to the stockroom — out of sight, out of mind.

Sometimes, I would bring out my favorite shoe, because maybe the next time they come in they'd like to try that pair. I'd ask them to try that pair on for my own satisfaction, so I could see how the shoe fit. We wouldn't pressure people because we wanted them to come back. Make sure they are happy when they walk out the door.

A "shoe dog" from the 1940s admires the merchandise.

Those were great days.

CHAPTER 8

CHARACTERS

In the early days of our company, many folks who sold shoes for us were a hard-living bunch. Oh, we also had a lot of God-fearing, churchgoing salesmen, but they weren't in the majority.

My dad was a real straight arrow. But he was also such a results-oriented person that if someone was a good salesman, my dad would put up with his peccadilloes — as long as the guy wasn't breathing booze in a customer's face. Everett didn't necessarily approve of that behavior, but he would tolerate it.

In the 1940s, Edison Brothers had a low-priced chain of shoe stores under the names Bakers, Leeds, and Chandler's. We're talking about shoes that retailed from $2 to $12. When I was running a shoe department, I used to recruit the best salesmen from those stores. I'd look through the window of those stores, and I could tell who was sharp and who was not. When a good salesman would leave his store for lunch, I'd go up to him and ask, "Did you ever think of going to work for Nordstrom?"

I eventually got into a little trouble doing that. But we'd usually have so many people applying for work here that we didn't have to resort to that kind of overt recruiting. We attracted good salespeople because we were doing the most business in town and, because we paid commission, they could make more money here. More important, we had a good reputation.

We had some really good salespeople who could sell a half-size off or a width off from what the customer should really have. They would stretch the shoe or put a slug (insole) in it to make it better. My dad didn't think much of those tricks. He wanted you to have the right item at the right price at the right time.

We had a lot of characters. My main-floor ladies' shoe buyer in Portland wore a full toupee, and it was not a good one. This fellow really wanted to be a nightclub comedian, but he couldn't get enough gigs so he became a shoe man. Every once in a while he would get a weekend gig. One time, before he went to work for us, he got a call from *The Ed Sullivan Show*, which was then one of the most popular programs on television. He had been a comedian on a cruise ship, and someone from the *Sullivan Show* had seen him and thought he was really funny. When a spot opened up on the show, they asked him to fill it, but because he was a "blue" comedian (he told dirty jokes), most of his act couldn't be performed on television in the 1950s.

I used to have a weekly management meeting in our lunchroom, first thing in the morning. One time, I looked at this fellow and noticed that the netting in his toupee was sticking up, but I didn't have the nerve to say anything. Turns out he was getting fitted for a new one, and they had been taking it off and putting it back on repeatedly.

One time, he and I went on a buying trip to New York, where we shared a hotel room with twin beds. He didn't want me to see that he was wearing a toupee, so he slept with it on. At the end of a long day, we both got into our respective beds and read for a while. I eventually turned out the light, said good night, and pretended to go to sleep. A few minutes later, I opened my eyes and saw him shutting his book and going into the bathroom. I heard the sound of his toupee coming off. He massaged his head for a while, put the toupee back on, and then got into bed, propped several pillows around his head, and didn't move for the rest of the night, because if he did, his toupee would be askew.

The bottom line was that he was a wonderful employee and a good friend.

Another guy, who worked on the second floor of the downtown Portland store, had to have all his teeth pulled. He bought a pair of false teeth at a drugstore but made the mistake of having them fitted while his mouth was still swollen. So when the swelling went down, the "choppers" no longer fit very well. Unfortunately, while waiting on a woman customer, he leaned over and his teeth fell out.

Tom Gardiner was a winner of the John W. Nordstrom Award, which is the highest honor in our company. He was my men's shoe manager and the only salesman in the men's department at the University store. Tom was one of the all-time greats, but he was a drinker. We sold a lot of shoe polish in our stores, and the shoe polish manufacturer would give a salesman a dime or a quarter for each container sold. Tom said, "My wife's been mad at me for drinking, so I'm only going to buy whiskey with my polish money." Well, he led the company in selling polish, so he had plenty of money to spend on booze.

We used to have company picnics at Vasa Park on Lake Sammamish, where there were some crazy moments amidst the softball games and three-legged races.

I'll never forget the time my mom and dad came down to Portland for a big company Christmas party at the Benson Hotel. We had a strict rule that men had to wear a suit at work. A fellow who we had just hired showed up at the party in the worst-looking sport coat and slacks — shockingly bad — and proceeded to ask my mother to dance, which was something she loved to do. She also loved to make conversation, so she couldn't avoid commenting on his unusual sport coat, but in a positive way. "My," she said, "that's quite a sport coat you have on. Where did you get it?"

To which he replied, "I made it myself. I learned how to sew in prison."

Those were great days.

Sharing a moment with my mother, Libby

The downtown Portland store in approximately 1969

Our performance there showed that we could operate outside Seattle, and that the Nordstrom **culture was transferable.**

CHAPTER 9

EXPANDING TO PORTLAND

In 1957, after a year as the main-floor ladies' shoe buyer in downtown Seattle, I was transferred to Portland. I was determined to be successful. In some ways, being the boss's son can be a hindrance because people think you were born with a silver spoon in your mouth. I was always very sensitive to that, so I just worked harder. For example, I — like all Nordstroms — picked up trash off the floor in the stores because when employees see the boss doing it, they realize that it would be good if they did, too.

Being the boss's son, and later being one of the bosses, I understood that I, like all of us Nordstroms, had a personal responsibility not to muddy the family name. There are many times when you are out socially and maybe would like to take one more drink, but if you're smart, you don't. You don't yell at your neighbor because his dog is dumping on your lawn. Seattle is a small town, where word gets around quickly.

When I first moved to Portland, I was single, and I wanted to live near the store so that I could spend as much time there as possible. One Sunday, I walked around downtown Portland looking for an apartment. I found this terrible-looking place and knocked on the manager's door. He showed me a one-room apartment with nothing but a bed and a Pullman kitchen. The price was right, and I said, "That's fine with me."

The night I moved in, I was lying in bed when all of a sudden, I heard this thump-thump-thump sound. I put on my clothes and went down the stairs — a different set of stairs from the ones I had walked up before. I came out on Jefferson Street and I found, right below my bedroom, a strip joint. I stayed in that place for a year before coming back to Seattle, and every night the sounds of ka-boom, ka-boom, ka-boom came rising up to my room.

Our expansion into Portland was a big deal for us. This was Lloyd's baby. Because Everett and Elmer had had their own accomplishments that were easily identifiable to them, Portland was Lloyd's opportunity to make his mark. He lived there for about four months to make sure that our business got off the ground successfully.

As our first store outside Seattle, Portland was our initial test of decentralization away from our hometown, and it was run as a business to serve the customers of Portland. Eventually our performance there showed that we could operate outside Seattle, and that the Nordstrom culture was transferable.

One of the first people in Portland who really understood our culture was a wonderful woman named Hazel Martin, who came to work in the Portland store about the same time I did. We became friends as well as co-workers, and we remain friends to this day. Hazel is still selling shoes in our downtown Portland store, and whenever I visit Portland, I make sure that I see her. I have a warm spot in my heart for Hazel, who is one of the very best in our company at developing a personal following. No one has more loyal customers than Hazel, who continues to represent the best and the essence of our culture.

Meier & Frank was a fabulous locally owned department store in Portland, not unlike Frederick & Nelson in Seattle. When we decided to open a big store and give the people of Portland the same kind of service we gave customers in Seattle, M&F responded by marking down by one-third every shoe that both of us carried. We responded by marking down the shoes one-third — less a dollar. That price war went on for one year. If we had been a public company then, we would have shown bad numbers. Eventually, they stopped doing it because they saw that we were in it for the long haul.

In 1960, I returned to Portland as general manager of our operations, which had expanded to a couple of leased shoe departments and three Nordstrom shoe stores. I replaced Harry Home, who early in 1960 decided to leave us and go into business for himself, in other areas of the shoe industry. I was well aware that I would be going up against hard sales numbers because Harry had done very well and everyone loved him.

Even after he left, Harry was still a part of Nordstrom and Nordstrom was a part of Harry. In later years, he would work for us on special assignments. He is a keeper of our culture, and I don't think anyone understands the basic elements of our culture better than he does. Even to this day, this big, handsome guy occasionally talks to our troops, and he still gets excited about waiting on people and doing the right thing.

By the way, I wasn't the only one who moved outside Seattle to manage a part of our business. John moved his family to Yakima and opened our first store there. Jim moved to Phoenix and managed the leased shoe departments at Rhodes Department Store. Jack moved to Portland to manage Nicholas Ungar, another apparel company that we purchased in the 1960s. Blake moved with his family to San Diego as a shoe buyer and later to Hillsdale, California, as a store manager. Pete relocated to Southern California two times: once as a shoe buyer at South Coast Plaza and later as the Orange County regional manager. Erik also moved a few times — first to South Coast Plaza as assistant manager in shoes and later to Minneapolis, where he opened our Mall of America store and served for several years as our regional/store manager. We continue to believe that moving to new areas, learning about a new marketplace and community, and working with different teams and leaders enriches the leadership experiences of our people. In fact, nearly all of our most successful leaders have had these kinds of experiences, and we believe they are better at their assignments for having had them.

As general manager, I supervised the buyers and went back to New York with them. I remember taking a trip to New York with Wes Harris, who was a buyer at that time. We were sitting on the floor in this sample room, picking out the hot shoes, and I commented to Wes, "You haven't picked out any blue shoes." He said he had, and he picked up a sample shoe. I said, "That isn't blue, that's green." It turned out that Wes was color-blind. I had a color-blind shoe buyer! Nevertheless, Wes was a wonderful, hardworking person — a John W. Nordstrom Award winner — and a lifelong good friend.

Unfortunately, in 2004, Wes was fatally injured after a fall from his Harley-Davidson motorcycle while riding back from Mount St. Helens with a group of friends. Wes, who was 70 at the time, was general manager of Bellevue Square, after a long, distinguished career in retail. He died doing something he loved, riding his Harley.

My wonderful family: Erik, Pete, Fran, Blake, and me

CHAPTER 10

A FAMILY OF MY OWN

As I mentioned, I was not the world's greatest college student. I liked the UW so much that, after four years, I found myself back in school for one more quarter, in order to get the credits I needed to graduate. Once I had completed my education, I was set to join the Army to fulfill my military obligation, which consisted of six months of active duty, then a two-week commitment every summer for seven years, usually in Yakima, Washington.

I needed to get a good grade in an economics class, but I hadn't paid much attention in class all semester, and I wasn't prepared to take the final exam. I needed somebody to explain to me what was going on, so I arranged with a girl in my class to study with her at her sorority house.

I rang the doorbell at the sorority house, the door opened, and standing in front of me was this beautiful girl. For me, it was literally love at first sight. I thought, wow. I loved her smile and everything about her.

Her name was Fran Wakeman. She had graduated from Franklin High in Seattle and was currently a freshman, doing door duty that night. I said I was looking for the girl from my economics class, and Fran told me where she was studying. I should have gone up to that room to study with that girl, but I didn't. I spent the whole evening talking to Fran while she answered the phone and did door duty.

Later that evening, I went back to my fraternity house and found a guy who had graduated from Franklin. I asked him if he knew Fran Wakeman. He did, and said, "She's one of the great gals from our class."

I said, "Could you fix me up?"

He did. We started going out, and pretty soon I'm in love. Unfortunately, she's not in love; she's in like. She felt that I was getting too serious. She was only a freshman, and she wanted to date more. That was depressing.

As a father, you don't want your kids growing up with a sense of entitlement.

Pretty soon, I left for the Army. In the meantime, Fran started going with another guy. Then I came back and we went out some more. This turned into an on-again, off-again thing for a couple of years. Because I was always working, I didn't have much time to pursue her.

Then she started going with a guy who had just graduated from dental school, so he was more educated than I was. He was handsome, and I'm not. He came from a well-to-do family, as did I, but I didn't have any money of my own and my parents were not going to give me any. He drove a fancy convertible, and I drove a beater. When I found out they were engaged, the news absolutely floored me.

The summer that Fran was going to get married, I was at Army Reserve camp in Yakima. I called home one day and my mother said, "Your grandmother would like to speak to you."

My grandmother got on the phone and said, "I just read in the paper that Fran has called off her engagement."

Turns out, one day before she was going to get married, she changed her mind. My future father-in-law had erected a tent in the backyard, cases of champagne on ice, the works. Her family had to post a notice in the newspaper so people would know not to go to the wedding. Fran later told me that she knew this guy was not for her. She had the guts to call off the wedding. I came home and we dated a little more, but at that point she was gun-shy, so we stopped seeing each other.

I was only 25, but I was already a conservative businessman and didn't want to look like a kid. I wore a hat (which in those days was a sign of maturity and gravitas) and was very serious about the business.

Around that time, Dave Tinling, a fraternity brother of mine, invited me to a party to celebrate his recent graduation from medical school. The party, at Dave's uncle's home in Broadmoor, was to start at five o'clock, but I had to work and told him that I couldn't get there until seven o'clock at the earliest. Anyway, I didn't feel up for a party. But he insisted that I come, so I said I would.

When I arrived at the party, it was overflowing with guests. I walked into the house, put down my hat, looked across the room, and there was Fran. We immediately made eye contact. Although we hadn't spoken for a long while, she rushed over to me with this big smile on her face, and we started talking, and talking, and talking. It was fabulous. But at this point, I was the one who was gun-shy. I was trying to keep her at arm's length, but she was just as friendly as could be. After a while, we both had a few glasses of wine, and continued talking in front of the fireplace. Although the room was crowded, it was as if nobody else was there.

A family portrait, 1966

Then she said to me, "I'll bet you something."

"What's that?"

"I'll bet you and I get married in the next six months."

So I guess she actually proposed to me, which was something I reminded her of many, many times over the years.

I ended up driving her home. I said, "I have to go to bed because I have to go to work. We're going to have lunch tomorrow and we'll discuss this."

I couldn't sleep all night. When she came to the store and we had lunch, I told her that our Half-Yearly Sale was coming up and I had several other things that I needed to attend to. So there was only a two-week window where we could get married.

Now, we're talking about all this in the light of day, which probably wasn't romantic, but she still said, "Okay!"

We did it. We got married in 1959, a mere two months after we rekindled our relationship. It was romantic and it was terrific.

RAISING THE BOYS

Our son Blake was born on October 4, 1960, followed by Pete on February 14, 1962. We later moved down to Portland, where Erik was born on October 24, 1963. Three boys in four years. I remember my mother asking me: "Do you not know where babies come from?"

When Fran and I were first married, Nordstrom was still a relatively small shoe business, but after a few years, we started to make some money. Fortunately, Fran and I inherited from both our families a conservative way of conducting oneself, so as our kids got older, and their friends were telling them that they had a lot of money, we kept material things in perspective. I always felt that we were fortunate to live on Mercer Island, where there were a lot of successful families with more money than we had. On Mercer Island, our kids were normal.

I believe that monetary wealth is often a destructive legacy to leave your children. As a father, you don't want your kids growing up with a sense of entitlement. If you are interested in your children as people and in their feelings of self-worth, you don't do them any favors by leaving them money that's not earned.

I can remember all three of my kids asking, "How come the so-and-sos get to go on lots of trips, and they're buying a new car, and a new boat?" I would say, "Because they've got more money than we do."

One of the things that I'm most thankful for is that, when they were teenagers, they put aside the fact that they had money. They said, "Okay, I've got that, but that's not me. I didn't earn that." All three of them said that to me at one time or another.

We gave them allowances when they were kids. But for any expenditure that was above and beyond what any kids get from their parents — clothes, etc. — they had to earn it. The first big one was the first car. When Blake turned 18, I proposed that he and his brothers and I each chip in to buy a car, splitting ownership four ways, and I volunteered to buy the insurance. We bought a used military-style jeep with a roll bar, which they thought was cool, and it was a great vehicle for Mercer Island, with all its winding roads. Part of my thinking was that the boys would rarely be able to drive very fast because by the time you shifted to high, you'd come to a turn and you'd have to downshift. I think I drove it twice, when it snowed, because it had four-wheel drive. They worked down at the store to make the money to pay for it, and they bought their own gas.

When each of them started working, at about age 12, I paid them in cash just as my dad did for me, but when they turned 15, they were on the payroll. Initially they were stockboys, which is dirty work. All three of them enjoyed being in the store, and they liked the camaraderie of working with the young people in our company. Salespeople are fun to be around.

I never pushed them to work in the store, but I did push them to work. One summer, Blake, who loves boats, worked for a shipbuilding operation, Vic Franck's Boat Company. He liked it until they gave him the worst job of all: cleaning out the holding tanks on some old boats. That day, he came home just white as a sheet, but he didn't quit. The funny thing about that was that the first holding tank he was assigned to clean out was on our own family boat, the *Fast Break.*

Regarding the name of the boat, when we first got it, I suggested a name for it: the *Slow Break*. At the time, I was playing basketball in a Slow Break League, where the rule is that when your side grabs a rebound, you can't cross the mid-court line until all five of the opposing team also cross the mid-court line. (Of course, they have to get across quickly.) So there's not a lot of running. When I said, "Let's call the boat the *Slow Break*," my three sons said, "We're never going to be on a slow break," so we called it the *Fast Break*.

Pete and Erik as Husky basketball players

I encouraged them to have interests outside of school. All my boys played Little League sports; Pete and Erik, who were pretty good athletes, played on teams at school. We were very committed to keeping our sons busy and out of trouble. I would often see kids that they knew hanging out at the drugstore after school. A lot of bad stuff can happen when you hang out with nothing to do.

Blake, God bless him, had my love of sports, but he also had my lack of talent. In high school, he became the manager of the Mercer Island basketball team. Blake's a big, strong fellow who knew all the guys on the team, and he was willing to pick up sweaty towels every afternoon in order to be part of that team. I give him tremendous credit for doing that; I'm not sure I could have done it. I think that, knowing I'm such a sports nut, he did it for me. Ed Pepple, the legendary basketball coach of Mercer Island High, said that Blake was the best manager he ever had, and I believe it. I was as proud of that as when Pete and Erik made the varsity.

The summer between Blake's sophomore and junior years, Ed organized a group of local players to go to Germany, England, and Holland to play against competition there, and he asked Blake to be the team manager. What a great growing experience for him. That summer, Blake left home a boy and came back a man.

Ed Pepple had a very positive influence on my kids. In an affluent community like Mercer Island, where the kids are used to having a lot, he has overcome much parental second-guessing and meddling. Ed was — and still is — a hard-nosed guy. It's either his way or the highway. Of course, he wins all the time, which really helps.

With Blake as manager, and Pete and Erik as players, I became close to the program, and got to know Ed very well. He and I would play tennis doubles together, and every year, we played the number one girls' tennis doubles team at Mercer Island High School. We even won a couple of times.

I think involvement in sports has been a key influence for my sons. It's a cliché, but it's true: Sports is a metaphor for life. You get humbled because there's always somebody better than you are. The best thing is that you have to struggle to make the team. You're not the star, no one is deferring to you, and you have to earn your playing time. Everything that you get, you worked hard to achieve. You learn to appreciate the value of sacrifice.

You learn to appreciate the
value of sacrifice.

Their sports experience has helped them as people and has helped them in this business. They are competitive guys. Today, running our company, they want to do something special on their watch. Even if they didn't get into this business, they would want to do something that was on their own hook.

I was a product of public schools, and I feel that you learn more about the real world by attending public schools, which is why I encouraged all three of them to do the same. I was certainly happy that they followed the family path to the UW, where Blake majored in economics, Erik in business administration, and Pete in English. I think Pete received the best education by learning to read, write, and speak well. He hadn't been much of a reader, then all of a sudden, he had to read these big Russian novels.

It's my belief that, for our business, the best education is on-the-job training. School certainly teaches you how to think, and it gives you the opportunity to mature a little bit while you're learning how to think.

When I turned 61, Pete gave me a list of things I had taught him, and had it framed. It is one of my favorite gifts.

Blake in the crew house at the University of Washington

THE TOP 20 THINGS MY DAD TAUGHT ME

(In No Particular Order)

• Effort and applying yourself is the most important thing.

• Boxers rather than briefs.

• Sports on TV is good.

• Be your brother's biggest supporter and best friend.

• Be sensitive to, and considerate of, your mother.

• Loyalty is an important quality.

• The shorter your hair the better.

• Don't spoil your dinner.

• If you can't say something nice, don't say anything at all.

• I ain't the son of no Stanley Marcus.

• Be respectful of people.

• Be a good neighbor.

• Take it inside, post up.★

• Never be critical of your family.

• Reading improves your fund of knowledge.

• Be thoughtful.

• Don't fit your shoes too short.

• Appreciate good music.

• Be good and if you can't be good, be careful.

• Don't be a turkey.★★

Love, Pete

[★set up near the basket to take a shot]

[★★That's what I'd call him when he lost his temper on the basketball court.]

Sports is a metaphor for life. You get humbled because there's *always somebody better than you are.* The best thing is that you have to struggle to make the team. You're not the star, no one is deferring to you, and you have to earn your playing time.

BLAKE NORDSTROM

Like all of us Nordstroms, Blake started his career in the stockroom and on the sales floor. He worked many summers and during college before making Nordstrom his career. With more than 20 years of experience, Blake is now president of the company.

We are the sum of our experiences. I feel so fortunate to have had two great parents. My mom raised us in a terrific way, and the two of them were on the same page. As a parent myself, I know that that's Rule Number One when it comes to raising kids.

Working in the store — which I did from the time I was about 11, sweeping floors, working in the stockroom — and continuing to this day, I feel so fortunate to have interfaced and had so many different experiences with so many different people, like Norm Sadis and Bob Nunn, who have helped make me who I am today.

Growing up, my brothers and I knew that our dad was really worried about spoiling us. But when we did something wrong, he never raised his voice to us. Instead, he would say, "I'm disappointed," and that felt like a knife in your side. You didn't want to disappoint him.

I've always felt his unwavering support of me. He was always in my corner. The funny thing is, as a kid, I had no concept of how hard he worked. I knew he worked a ton of hours at the store, of course, but I also knew that family came first with him. So many of my friends would make the comment to me: "My dad doesn't work as many hours as your dad, but my dad isn't as available as your dad."

Growing up, I always liked mechanical things, like mini-bikes and go-karts. I especially liked boats, so we got into boating when I was 12 or 13, and we bought a 36-footer. I maintained it, cleaned it, and even got gas for it. One time at a party, a friend of my dad came up to him and said, "Bruce, I don't want to tell on Blake, but just so you know, I saw him driving your boat." My dad said, "That's right; he's in charge."

One time, I hit a log and bent the prop. My dad just said to me, "Are you okay?" Yes, I am. "Did you learn something?" Yes. "Then good."

PETE NORDSTROM

Pete is now president of merchandising for the company. He also spent many years learning the business, from the stockroom to the sales floor to buying and management positions in various regions.

At work, I always felt that my dad was in my corner, and he never second-guessed me. I remember the time when I was the store manager in Tacoma, and somebody wanted to return a pair of jeans that were obviously well worn. I told the customer that we wouldn't accept the return. Darrel Hume, a Nordstrom employee I once worked with, told me that when it comes to returns, "Everything has to pass a test of reasonableness." In my opinion, in that case, it wasn't reasonable.

The customer was angry and said he wanted to speak to my boss, and he ended up talking to my dad. Dad wanted to do what was right for the customer, but that desire was overwhelmed by his desire to be supportive of his son. The customer was letting my dad have it about his horrible experience with me, and my dad just wasn't having it. He said, "Look, if that's what Pete told you, that's the way it's going to be."

He later talked to me about the incident and told me that I should have taken the return, but he was not going to let anybody else tell me that.

He's much more interested in being our dad than being our boss. Growing up, I just wanted him to be proud of what I was doing. When we talk, the subjects of business and work obviously come up because they are so much a part of our lives, but we generally don't talk a lot about specific business issues. He wants to be our dad. When we have lunch, we would sooner talk about the Sonics or the Huskies than about the gross margins in women's apparel. Now in retirement, he's still vitally interested in the business, but our relationship is much more about his being a supportive father who is proud of his sons.

ERIK NORDSTROM

Erik is now president of stores, working alongside his brothers. Like them, Erik learned the business by working summers in the stockroom and selling shoes. He later worked in several regions in management positions before returning to Seattle.

Reputation is very important to my dad. I was 12 years old the first summer I came to work at the store, starting in the stockroom, along with Pete. That same summer, Blake started selling. We were obviously not the most inconspicuous of employees. Dad talked to us about how to conduct ourselves and the importance of reputation, but I was 12 years old, and I wasn't worrying about my reputation.

To Dad, our reputation started with being hard workers, which was more important to him than being the best salesperson. He didn't want us to be perceived as the spoiled kids of the boss.

I wasn't that conscious of our image within the company until I graduated from college and went to work in our store at South Coast Plaza, where I started my career as the co-third assistant manager of the women's shoe department.

Working as a team is perfectly natural for my brothers and me. My dad believes that supporting your family is the most important thing you can do. I never heard him say anything negative about his cousins. They didn't always agree, but they supported whatever the group decided.

My brothers and I have worked together many times. When I was a salesperson, Blake became my manager; when I was a buyer, he became my merchandiser; when I was a store manager, he became my regional manager. He never hired me; I was already in those jobs when he got those promotions. It was always the best working for my brother because he had more confidence in me and gave me more autonomy than anybody I had ever worked for. But he also had higher expectations than anybody I had ever worked for. He believed in me more than I believed in myself. I didn't want to let him down.

Ed has coached the Mercer Island High School basketball team for more than four decades, and is the all-time winningest high school coach in the state of Washington. He coached Pete and Erik, and selected Blake to be the team manager.

Blake was never going to be an outstanding athlete, but he impressed me as a young guy who had great character and an excellent work ethic, and he became as good a manager as I ever had. I didn't have to worry about any of the details because Blake took care of everything. A manager has to take down the baskets in the gym, bring out the basketballs, sweep the floor, inventory and organize the equipment, and keep records of it. During the practices and the games, he has a ton of other stuff to do.

I think being a manager helped Blake with the team concept. He was a contemporary, a peer of all the guys on the team, who respected him. You can look at the job of manager as being a servant, or you can look at it as being part of the team, which is how Blake saw it.

The Nordstrom boys weren't naturally gifted athletes, but they worked so hard, they made themselves as good as possible.

Pete was a "blue-collar" guy. You knew he was going to give you the best he had every single time he was out on the court. When he was a senior, we had a gifted group of sophomores who played ahead of him, but he was a team guy and sublimated his ego.

Erik was the best player. When that gifted group of sophomores became seniors, he played with them as a junior. He was versatile and could adapt to any playing situation.

The third generation

Loyalty is at the heart of any success
we've had, and it is the personality trait
that I value the highest.

CHAPTER II

OUR TURN

In the late 1950s, we added 20,000 square feet to our downtown Seattle store by taking over the first three floors and basement of the Ranke Building, and then adding more street-level space when Weisfield's Jewelers moved to another location downtown. The remodeling took a couple of years, and by March 1959, we had a grand opening of what was then the country's largest shoe store, stocked with more than 100,000 pairs of shoes on four floors of selling space.

We installed a shoe-shine stand by the front door, which at that time was an unusual feature, and for almost 35 years, we kept the shines at 25 cents because it attracted people to the store.

Over the next couple of years, we opened stores in Bellevue Square, across Lake Washington from Seattle; Yakima, Washington; Lloyd Center, outside Portland; and Aurora Village, north of Seattle, and continued to learn how best to operate additional stores and how to identify the right managers to run those stores. We discovered that our system generated more good managerial candidates than the systems in other stores. Because we tend to allow good salespeople to do things on their own initiative, we developed a large cadre of good people who could become managers, helping us to expand the business.

By the early 1960s, Everett and Elmer were gradually phasing out their day-to-day involvement in the business, allowing Lloyd to run the company as chairman. I reported directly to Lloyd. Everett and Elmer, who had great respect for Lloyd, felt that because he came into the business later, he didn't get the recognition that they got. That was one of the major reasons why they kept their hands off the business and rarely showed up at the store.

One day, while I was still working in Portland, Lloyd called me about returning to Seattle to become president of the company. He told me that I had what it takes to be president. When you're 30 years old, that vote of confidence means a lot.

My dad wouldn't be the one calling me about becoming president because he didn't want this promotion to smack of favoritism. I was older than my cousins John and Jim, and had been working in the business longer than they and Jack McMillan had. Although Jack is older than I am, he didn't start in the business until after he had served in the U.S. Navy for a couple of years before completing college at the UW.

I came back to Seattle in early 1963, after the Seattle World's Fair, and assumed the role of president. Although Everett, Elmer, and Lloyd ran the company as a committee, Lloyd didn't think that would work for my generation. Later on, I'll talk about how my cousins and I eventually came to share the power and decision-making responsibilities on our watch.

It isn't easy to pass on a family business to the next generation. As we were growing up in the business, there were many other independent shoe retailers around the country. Most of the larger ones were members of Shoes Associated, an effective trade organization made up of the leading independents. We met once a year with fellow members of Shoes Associated, and had lots of telephone conversations; we compared notes and helped each other. I learned a lot by talking to these guys.

Nevertheless, in the ensuing years, just about all of them failed. Most of them were family-run businesses that were led by people with strong personalities and a great work ethic, but for whatever reason, they couldn't pass the business on to the next generation, nor were they able to successfully promote a non-family member to leadership. In classes I taught at the University of Washington Business School, I advocated the committee system because that's what we did. But most experts will tell you not to be run by a committee because, in most cases, it doesn't work, and over the years, I've come to realize that the experts are generally right. We were, I guess, the exception to the rule.

LOYALTY

During this time, there were three shoe guys I worked very closely with, and with whom I'm still close: Norm Sadis, Bob Nunn, and Ernie Carino. They all started out on the sales floor and eventually became our top managers. If something went wrong with their business, there wasn't much conversation. They just turned around and went back and got after it.

Bob Nunn joined us in 1965 in Tacoma and worked his way up through the ranks with his characteristic bulldog tenacity, which is a personality trait that I greatly admire. Bob was a champion of empowerment, of pushing decision-making down to the sales floor. He was somebody who wasn't frightened by smart people. He knew that by surrounding himself with strong, smart people, he would get better results.

Norm Sadis, who began selling shoes at our store in 1962, when he was just 18, was such a great salesman, with a burning desire to sell everybody a pair of shoes. Good salesmen don't necessarily make good managers, but Norm was as good at running a department as anybody I ever saw, in addition to being an excellent buyer — a rare combination.

Ernie Carino also came to work for us at age 18, in 1961, in the basement of Rhodes in Tacoma. At a time when he was working for us in the Seattle store, my father asked Ernie to drop off a jar of shoe polish for a customer on Mercer Island, on his way home to Tacoma. It was a dark, rainy night, and as Ernie was trying to find the customer's home in his beat-up Chevy, he wondered why Mr. Everett would waste his time delivering a 25-cent jar of shoe polish. But he did it, and the experience made an impression on him. Ernie learned that it wasn't about the size of the purchase; it was about taking care of the customer.

When Ernie was about 21, he was walking the stockroom of the downtown store with my dad, who was advising him on a series of things he should be doing with the inventory. As my dad talked, Ernie kept nodding and saying, "Uh-huh, uh-huh, uh-huh." Then my dad said to him: "Ernie, you must be a lot smarter than I am because I can't remember everything I'm talking to you about. I have to write it all down." Ever since that day, Ernie has always carried around a yellow tablet to write things down. Norm Sadis and Bob Nunn do, too.

Ernie rose through the ranks to become my right-hand man. In 1973, after 11 years, he decided to leave the company. That was like somebody throwing a bucket of cold water on me.

I said, "Are you going to work for a competitor?"

He said, "I would never work for a competitor. I'm going into the construction business."

Loyalty is at the heart of any success we've had, and it is the personality trait that I value the highest. Ernie was a loyal guy.

Golfing with Norm Sadis, Ernie Carino, and Bob Nunn

You can't order people to be loyal, just as you can't make them do something they don't want to do. For example, when I was in the Army, this colonel came into our outfit and announced, "Gentlemen, starting today, every one of you will smile and you will enjoy it." No we won't. You can't make people smile; they have to smile from the inside.

I'm loyal to my alma mater, the University of Washington, which I think is a fabulous asset to our city and our state, and I will always support the school with my time and money. In terms of Husky sports, I'm not a fair-weather fan. I'm as much a Husky football fan when they win one game in a season as I am when they go undefeated.

I've already talked about how much I treasure the experiences I had, and the friendships I made, during my fraternity days at Beta Theta Pi. A while back, the Beta house at the UW was going through a difficult period; the brothers were regularly getting into trouble and the fraternity was losing membership. Many angry alums wanted to close up the house and sell it. I didn't want that to happen and neither did Bud Erickson, my old fraternity brother, who was our director of store planning. Both Bud and I had gotten so much out of living in the house, and we wanted other people to have that chance. We got a lot of alums involved, and we were able to raise over $1 million, which was darn hard in an atmosphere where half the people didn't want to give you one cent. We fixed up the house, kicked out many of the guys in the fraternity, and today, we're the best house on the campus. I'm very proud of that, and I'm proud of those kids.

How does that feeling of loyalty translate to our business? Like every other retailer, we have turnover, but ours happens right after someone is hired. Sink or swim. There are some sinkers — not to mention stinkers — out there, and we wash 'em out pretty darn fast.

But if somebody sticks with us a while, then our loyalty to them increases, and their loyalty to us increases. The retail industry is famous for musical chairs of buyers, merchandise managers, and executives, but we very rarely lose a key person to a competitor, which is something I'm really proud of. I think it's an indication that the people we are associated with are loyal to us.

When Betsy Sanders, who was one of our superstars, left the company, she told me, "I will never work for another retailer."

When Betsy, Harry Home, Norm Sadis, Ernie Carino, and Bob Nunn left, it was sad because they were important people in our organization. But I have been here long enough to tell you that even when the superstars leave, somebody steps up to take their place.

JACK MCMILLAN

Jack joined our team after graduating from the University of Washington. He quickly took on many responsibilities and continued to be a part of our team until we retired.

In 1957, I was working my way through the University of Washington on the GI Bill and was employed at Washington Mutual Savings Bank. At that time, my father-in-law, Lloyd Nordstrom, asked me to work in the shoe store instead of the bank. His pitch was "No matter how bad the economic cycle, people always buy shoes."

I took his advice. I went to school in the morning and sold shoes in the afternoon. After graduation, I began selling shoes full-time.

I started on the budget floor, where most shoes sold from $5 to $10, and I was eventually promoted to the main floor, where we sold shoes all the way up to $29.99. It was hard to tell the customer that price because it was a lot of money at that time.

Whenever it got busy in the children's or teenage department, they would call for help, and we salespeople on the main floor would have to go upstairs to assist with lower-priced sales. One day, I got a call to go up to children's shoes, and my first thought was "I'm a main-floor shoe salesman." The last thing I wanted to do was spend a lot of time trying to sell kids' shoes for five or six bucks. I wanted to sell the higher-priced main-floor shoes because I needed the money from commissions.

So I went upstairs, sold one pair of children's shoes, then slipped back downstairs to the main floor. Somehow, Lloyd found out about it. He called me up into the office and just chewed me out because I wasn't appreciating the big picture. He said, "Jack, you can't be selfish. When we have a need in the store and you're called upstairs, you stay upstairs."

I said, "Yes, sir," saluted, went back down to the sales floor, and never did it again. Lloyd was right; we all need to appreciate the big picture, not just our own individual deal. That was a great lesson to learn, and Lloyd Nordstrom was a great man who was always very supportive of me.

ERNIE CARINO

Ernie started at Nordstrom in 1961, the same year he turned 18, graduated from high school, and got married. He rose through the management ranks until he left the company in 1973 to go into the construction business.

Because of financial reasons, I never had the opportunity to go to college, so when people asked me what college I went to, I'd say, "The University of Nordstrom." I couldn't have gotten a better on-the-job college education, not only in the retail shoe business, but also in the people business.

Bruce was my mentor, and he was more like a teammate than a boss. He was like the quarterback on the football team, and we were all on the same team, with the same goals: to get the right product and to take care of the customer.

When Nordstrom first merged with Best's Apparel, their people didn't understand how Nordstrom did things. For the Half-Yearly Sale, we had always opened the store an hour early because we had big numbers to make. I was in charge of the shoe division in our store. When I told the Best's store manager, who ran apparel, what I was going to do, he said, "I'm not going to open early just for your shoe sale."

We shoe dogs were not as sophisticated as the apparel people. I said, "I feel very strongly, so I'm going to do this." We had figures to meet, and I didn't want to lose that extra selling time.

I called Bruce and told him. His answer was: "Well, what are you going to do?"

I said I planned to rope off the shoe division, open up the main door coming out of the mall (where all the people come in), and funnel them through to the shoe department. He told me to do it, and supported my decision. That taught me to go ahead, follow your passion, don't just lie down and die. By the time of the following year's Half-Yearly event, we were one store, one company.

BOB NUNN

Bob started at Nordstrom in 1965 and rose through the ranks, eventually becoming an executive vice president. He was one of our top shoe dogs.

We learned early on that you have to show respect for your product, your customer, and every part of your business. When we brought that shoe out to the customer, it was tissued right, and it showed you had respect for the merchandise. The Nordstroms believed that there was a lot of money in those boxes.

The first thing I learned as a manager was to hire and keep the smartest and strongest people I could find. In hiring, we didn't ask about their education. I always looked for somebody who was a little hungry because that's what I was when I joined the company. I wanted somebody who was eager to get ahead, to reach that next plateau.

Our philosophy was to let people take their business and run with it. Giving people the freedom to run their own department enabled them to achieve more than they could have in another company, where they would have been told what to do every day. Was it perfect all the time? No. But it was more perfect than wrong most of the time.

Norm Sadis, Ernie Carino, and I worked very closely with Bruce throughout our careers, and we were close to him personally as well. For Bruce's 70th birthday, we took him on a golf trip to Bandon Dunes in Oregon, and we presented him with a putter, which was engraved with the words that summed up the way we did business at Nordstrom: "Never compromise."

Norm started with the company in 1962 and became one of our leading shoe dogs.

We learned early how to greet the customer, seat the customer, measure both feet, go to the stockroom, and bring out a minimum of four pairs of shoes. If you couldn't sell the customer, they wanted you to turn it over to someone else because the sale was very important.

When the customer left, you were to put the shoes away in a certain way. You had to tissue the shoes properly and put them back in this massive stockroom (although not nearly as massive as it is today).

Jay Hansen, our manager, used to watch what we were doing as far as taking care of the customer. When you went to the stockroom, he followed you to see if you put the shoes away properly. I remember him catching me tissueing the shoes incorrectly, and he said, "We're going to make sure you never forget how to tissue a pair of shoes. You see that section over there? (There were more than 100 pairs of shoes in each section.) Before you go home tonight, I want you to go through that section and make sure every pair of shoes is tissued correctly."

The Nordstroms ingrained in us that this was our business. We knew that the profit-sharing program was the way that we were going to save for tomorrow. Every time we did something to help the company profits, it would come back to benefit us. Every dime we saved, we got part of it. For example, all of us shoe dogs carried shoehorns, and when we left the store at night, we would put our shoehorns in a box by the door.

Bruce entrusted us with his kids when they came to work at the store. When everyone else's kids were traveling somewhere at Christmas or Easter, these kids were working. When Blake started selling shoes on the floor, we carried Clinic nursing shoes, which was a basic, so you didn't want to be out of sizes. Sure enough, he went home one day after work and told his dad, "I missed a size 7B." The next day, the phone rang; it was Bruce, telling me about that. Later, I said to Blake, "What happens at the store stays in the store."

CHAPTER 12

OUR MOVE INTO APPAREL

My generation was coming on and we needed to grow. The question among us was whether to grow our shoe business out of the Pacific Northwest, where we were already doing a lot of business, or diversify and buy a local business where the Nordstrom name was already well known.

In 1963, our family made the decision to acquire Best's Apparel, a fashion-forward women's apparel retailer with stores in Seattle and Portland. Its motto was "Specialists in smart apparel for young women of all ages."

Buying Best's was one of the watershed events in the history of our company. It was Lloyd's idea. As Elmer recalled in his book, *A Winning Team*, "Lloyd had the feeling, because he came in late, that he didn't have as strong a part in building the business as the two of us, which was a mistake, of course."

The decision to buy Best's was not a slam dunk; it was preceded by a long family discussion. But Lloyd's enthusiasm for the deal (he had been negotiating with Dorothy Cabot Best for four years) ultimately swayed Everett and Elmer to vote for it. Our generation thought it was a great challenge and opportunity.

Mrs. Best, who had recently passed away, was an excellent merchant, but her husband, Ivan, was an accountant with zero feel for the fashion business, which is why their family sold the business to our family.

It wasn't as if Nordstrom and Best's was an ideal fit. Our styles of business could not have been more different. While we were a bunch of hustling shoe dogs, Best's catered to the fashion-forward and better-apparel business.

Buying Best's was one of the watershed events in the history of our company.

Bob Bender, circa 1963

I remember visiting the Best's store on Fifth and Pine in Seattle after we had bought the company. I took the elevator to the second floor and looked around. There was not one stitch of clothing on display, not a hanger or a ring-around. Nothing. Just velvet curtains and a settee. And sitting in a high-back chair watching the elevator was this stern-looking woman who appeared to be evaluating my worthiness to be on the premises.

I came to find out that this was a salon. There would be nothing so gauche as having merchandise out on the floor where you could see it. If you passed muster with the woman in the high-back chair, she would take you into the back room and start bringing out the wares. Not exactly the Nordstrom way.

After buying Best's, we had tremendous resistance from vendors, who thought of us as a bunch of shoe clerks who had stumbled their way into the apparel business. The first really powerful national brand we persuaded to join us was Estée Lauder, the cosmetics line, which was a landmark deal for us. Estée Lauder gave us credibility, broke the dam of industry resistance, and allowed other vendors to take a more positive look at us.

We made our share of mistakes, but they worked out to our benefit. For example, we dramatically overbought. We were shoe guys who were used to turning over inventory twice a year (and we made money doing that). In apparel, on the other hand, you can turn inventory nine or ten times a year. We ultimately learned that you must turn apparel often in order to limit markdowns. Intellectually, we knew that fashion apparel "spoils" fast, but our merchant blood flowed differently and more emotionally, so we just loaded up the inventory in that store. If it was February and you wanted a raincoat, we had a lot of raincoats, as opposed to other stores that didn't have any, even though it was right in the heart of the raincoat season; they had sold out all their raincoats by December. If you wanted a bathing suit in June, we had a lot of bathing suits. Again, the other stores were already sold out. But we were successful with that approach.

We always tried to have a broad-based business, to pick up business on the edges. Consequently, nobody else in town would carry size 13 women's shoes or size 20 men's. We just beat them all to heck if they tried to do it.

If you take care of people who are hard to fit or hard to satisfy, they become your emissaries, your best advertising. In fact, we've always felt that conventional advertising of all kinds is overvalued in our industry, and that the best advertising is word of mouth. Today, we do less newspaper advertising and more direct-mail and fashion-magazine advertising, which adds to the aura and reputation of the company. But our advertising budget is about 2 percent of our total sales; by comparison, most department stores allocate over 5 percent. We feel that if you make your ad budget lean, your people will think more about how they spend the money in the budget, and therefore, you should get more bang for your buck.

As my dad once said, "I know half this advertising money is going down a rat hole. I just don't know which half."

SELL, SELL, SELL

At the time we acquired Best's, we were still a private business, so there was no scorecard being kept on us, except by our bankers, who didn't like all this inventory we were buying. But we had a lot of ammunition in our stores, and boy, did we do business! We had trouble getting the numbers to the bottom line, but we did well on the top line.

To us Nordstroms, sales were the thing. Get those sales up! When you do that, a lot of your fixed costs come down dramatically.

At the end of the first year, we had lost money, but we were heroes to the consumers in Seattle and Portland.

If you take care of people who are hard to fit or hard to satisfy, they become your emissaries, your best advertising.

To this day, we have always been adamant about not being undersold, and bringing the best value we can to the customer. Value is not necessarily just the price of something; it's what you get for your money. We offer many of the same brands that the competition offers — at the same or lower price — plus the added value of better service and a beautiful store environment. We do not use our ancillary costs as an excuse to charge more money. We will not be undersold.

Most vendors who were selling to us didn't care whether we made money (which is very shortsighted because we're all in this together). They did care that almost immediately after we got into apparel, we went to the top of the list in terms of annual sales per square foot.

We were really good at the juniors business. My cousins and I were young ourselves, so we had a natural interest in that business. At Best's the juniors' department was called "Miss B's Place," which we eventually changed to Brass Plum. We made a meal of that juniors business. We knew that we could have these customers for the rest of their lives if we did the job right.

It took a little longer to change the culture at the point of sale, to where salespeople had that urgency that we think is essential to being a Nordstrom person. It took a good year to change that culture. Those were great days, and a lot of fun.

When we started in apparel, all we had was women's. Best's had one counter on the main floor for men's products such as ties and shirts — mainly the kind of stuff that women would buy for men. But early on in the game, we began to conceive a men's and children's business to complement our shoes. Shoes are an accessory, but we bought the apparel to make sure that we maintained our existing strong shoe business.

After we bought Best's, there was a lot of discussion about what to call our company. Because we didn't know much about apparel, we needed to have Best's, which was well known in Seattle and Portland, as part of our name. In 1969, we officially changed our name to Nordstrom Best. As soon as we felt confident, we dropped "Best" from our name.

BOB BENDER

Among the many mistakes we made early on was looking to hire someone who was an expert in women's ready-to-wear. We did a lot of due diligence in our search. Lloyd went back to Seventh Avenue and talked to a lot of different people.

We eventually hired a fellow to be the head merchandise manager for our better women's apparel. He was good at putting on fashion shows, which earned us a lot of credit with customers. But when we found out how much money he was spending on those shows, we asked him to cut back, which offended him.

It soon became obvious that he was disdainful of our way of doing business. One morning, I was giving a pep talk at a meeting and I said, "Next month, we've got to go for the gusto. We're going to sell stuff. We're going to break records. We're going to have increases. We're going to have a steak-and-bean-dinner contest between this half of the room of managers vs. the other half. (Having a contest was our answer to everything.) The winners are going to eat steak, and the losers are going to eat beans and will have to serve the steaks to the winners."

You could just see the fire coming out of these people. Let's go get 'em!

I thought I had done a pretty good job. I was walking out of the room right behind this guy, who didn't see me. He turned to the fellow next to him and said, "Wasn't that the most sophomoric thing you've ever heard?"

I thought, "He's probably right. But he doesn't get it."

Sure enough, he didn't last much longer. His department had world-record low gross margins. By the way, he went back East and worked for a variety of big companies in very fancy jobs. But he wasn't for us.

It was obvious that we needed to find someone who understood our culture, who approached the business the way we did, who had our work ethic, and who could be trusted to run this. We were all shoe guys, so we needed to look outside our organization.

The guy we wanted was Bob Bender, who lived in our neighborhood in Seattle. His dad ran a men's haberdashery in town, and Bob was a star of the downtown J.C. Penney store, which was then on Second and Pike.

With Fran, at the party celebrating our purchase of Best's Apparel

The decision to buy Best's was not a slam dunk; it was preceded by a long family discussion. Our generation thought it was a great **challenge** and **opportunity.**

We knew that Bob was hardworking, squeaky clean, and honest. When I was working at Rhodes, across the street from Penney's, I saw that Bob had set up a card table right out on the sales floor, where he could do his paperwork and still see what was going on.

Bob joined us in 1965. Before hiring him, we had never brought in anybody from outside the company. He built our main-floor business, including accessories, handbags, cosmetics, and small leather goods.

It was almost impossible to work harder than Bob Bender, who had a sense of urgency about getting the job done. He worked his tail off and set a great pace for the work ethic in this company. Stories about him are legendary at Nordstrom. Once a year, he would take four women's buyers to Europe on buying trips. They would rent a car, drive all night from city to city, from Germany to France to Italy, and stay in very inexpensive hotels. The young buyers all went through the test of fire with him on those European buying trips. It was a great lesson for all of us — how much he cared and how hard he worked, and how much people admired and loved him. Bob, who contributed so much to our business and our culture, retired as vice chairman in 1992, after 27 years with our company.

Bob also oversaw our gift department. The original gift department at Best's was subpar, but Lloyd and I thought gifts could be a good complement to our clothes and shoes. Lloyd said that Neiman's had the best gift department, bar none, so I cold-called Stanley Marcus, the legendary chairman of Neiman Marcus, and asked if I could come down and visit his store. He said, "You're a shoe guy. That's how I got started in this business. Come on down."

I flew to Dallas with our new gifts buyer and was met at the store by Stanley. He introduced my buyer to his buyer, and the two of them went off on their own. Stanley took me on a tour of their downtown Dallas flagship store, and we had lunch together in the executive dining room. He could not have been nicer to a kid in his thirties. I don't think he thought Nordstrom would ever be a competitor of Neiman Marcus. Stanley Marcus was just like Jeffrey Kalinsky, in whose two Jeffrey stores we acquired a majority interest in 2005. At the heart of both their enterprises is giving good service.

BOB BENDER

Bob started with us in 1965, just about a year after Nordstrom acquired Best's, and became one of the most important executives in the history of our company, before retiring in 1992.

When I left J.C. Penney to come to Nordstrom, I discovered that Nordstrom had no type of inventory control. There was so much apparel that I was overwhelmed. It appeared to me that they wanted to carry the same level of heavy inventories in apparel as they had in shoes, which was an entirely different business.

At the time, Nordstrom belonged to a national buying group of specialty stores. Every year, we would have meetings with those stores, who considered us a bunch of country bumpkins. When they came out to Seattle to evaluate the apparel operation a few years after we acquired Best's, they were appalled at what they saw. They questioned the quantity of inventory and the taste level in some departments. After all, they were the experts and we were the novices. Some of them were pretty snooty. Nordstrom has always tried to appeal to a broad base, and carrying all that inventory helped build the sales. Because we had the selection, customers came to our stores.

Another extremely important part of the Nordstrom story was when Everett, Elmer, and Lloyd visited Neiman Marcus to look at their customer service, which was without a doubt the best in the country. They came back to Seattle and talked to Bruce, John, Jim, Jack, and me about customer service. When the five of us later visited Neiman's to see for ourselves, I played the part of a customer to see how I was taken care of, and it was fabulous. It was all about taking care of the customer and making the customer feel at home. Never say no; nothing is impossible. That experience laid the groundwork for what Nordstrom became.

ALLAN GOESLING

Allan started working for Nordstrom on January 6, 1952, as the company's chief financial officer. After he retired in 1980, he was succeeded by his son John. Father and son combined to run our finance department for 50 years.

After answering a newspaper ad for the job, I had my first interview with Everett, Elmer, and Lloyd. Going into that interview, I didn't know much about them. But I can tell you this: When you got through with the interview, you knew you had been grilled. It was a real experience.

They were all very nice, but they asked some penetrating questions to try to understand me. I asked them questions about the company, what their strategy was, etc. It was a nice interview that lasted over an hour. When I got home, I said to my wife, "I don't know if I'm going to hear from them or not. I don't think I gave them all the answers they were looking for."

I later had a second interview with Everett and Lloyd (Elmer was in Phoenix recovering from surgery), and right then they offered me a job.

Each of them had a nickname: Everett was Whitey, Elmer was Sparky, and Lloyd was Pinky.

There was no politicking with them. You always knew where you stood. If there was something they didn't like, they came out and told you in a very nice way. You understood where they were coming from, and you knew exactly what they wanted.

Buying Best's Apparel: The day after the deal was made, Everett called me on the telephone and said, "We are going to see Mr. Franklin at the bank because we have to borrow some money." Chuck Franklin, president of Pacific National Bank, our main bank on Second Avenue, was Everett's fraternity brother at the UW, and a close friend. The next morning, Everett walked into Franklin's office and told him that we had bought Best's Apparel and needed to borrow some money. Franklin asked, "How much do you need?" Everett told him $1 million, and Franklin opened his desk, pulled out a note, filled it in, and had Everett sign it. Franklin said, "The money will be in your bank account today."

employee
handbook

Welcome to Nordstrom.
We're glad to have you with our Company.

Our number one goal is to provide outstanding customer service.
Set both your personal and professional goals high.
We have great confidence in your ability to achieve them,
so our employee handbook is very simple.

We have only one rule...

our
one
rule

Use good judgment in all situations.

Our employee handbook

CHAPTER 13

OUR REPUTATION

We pride ourselves on our reputation for customer service, which goes all the way back to my grandpa's day. Some people may think that the idea for giving good service suddenly came to us in a flash of light, but that was not the case. Our reputation for service is the result of an evolutionary process that spans the history of our company. Why have we emphasized service? It's very simple. Over the years, we learned that the more service we provided, the better our business became. It's no more complicated than that.

With that reputation comes great responsibility. We certainly realize that every day, there are times when we don't live up to that reputation. In fact, right now, there is something going on in one of our stores that would give me an ulcer. I know that firsthand because I often wander around some of our out-of-town stores, where they don't know who I am. (That's not surprising. After all, we have over 50,000 employees.) One time, I was in California visiting one of our stores that does a ton of business, and I saw a shoe salesman and a shoe saleswoman laughing and giving each other high fives.

She went to the back room and I walked up to the salesman. I said, "Let me introduce myself. I'm Bruce Nordstrom."

He nervously asked me how I was doing. I said, "Not very well. When you're fooling around on the floor, think of what the customer thinks when they're looking at you."

I didn't talk to the store manager. I didn't turn him in. It was between him and me. I can be the bad guy so the store manager doesn't have to be the bad guy.

We understand completely that our customers are deserving of kindness, attention, and professionalism.

About 15 years ago, I went to a Christmas service at the University Presbyterian Church, which is a huge place that seats hundreds of people. We love to go there at Christmas for the singing, and we love to sing. The minister used Nordstrom in his sermon about serving, calling it "The Gospel According to Nordstrom." I was so flattered, I wrote him a letter of thanks.

To us, service is an honorable thing. Service is about elevating the person you are waiting on, making that person feel better about the shopping experience. We understand completely that our customers are deserving of kindness, attention, and professionalism.

In being committed to service, we have learned that you can't judge customers by the way they are dressed. At a store we once operated in Fairbanks, Alaska, the door opened one day and the snow blew in, along with a guy in a big insulated suit that was filthy, greasy, dirty. His hair was coming out of his hat. He looked like a wild man. Many people would have wanted to kick him out of the store, but our people up there understood the situation. The customer had been working up in the oil fields of the Arctic Circle, where they work nine months on and three months off. He had just returned from his stint, and came into the store right off the plane. He ended up buying a lot of clothes, and the salesman made a lot of money. I found out about this because I was looking at the daily sales figures and saw that little Fairbanks had had this huge day. I called them up and they told me the story.

Because our reputation is fragile, we must take care of every customer. Otherwise, unhappy customers will tell people how they were mistreated in our store. Conversely, if you can give them good service, they could be customers for life. They may not have any money now, but maybe they will someday. Maybe their kids will be customers of ours. Everybody has got to be served.

We keep raising the bar ourselves. Maybe the toughest place for us to do business is Seattle, where we have been at it since 1901. When one of our people in Seattle is rude or doesn't serve somebody well, we hear about it, right away.

On the other hand, when we go to new cities, we get all these wonderful letters from people telling us they've never been served like this before. But I know that often when we go to new areas, we are probably not performing at the same level that we do here. When Betsy Sanders opened up Southern California for us in 1978, she was one of the few who turned it up instantly. We have since discovered that it generally takes some time to build up that kind of momentum.

THE WAY WE HANDLE RETURNS

One of our company's most important values is trust. We want our customers to trust us, to trust doing business with us, and to know that if they have a problem with the merchandise they have purchased from Nordstrom, we will work to find a solution. How we handle returns has evolved since the days of Everett, Elmer, and Lloyd. As Elmer once said, "We decided to let the clerks [as they were referred to in his day] make the adjustments, so they would be the fair-haired boys."

When I worked at Rhodes, I was embarrassed every time there was an adjustment because the customer had to go stand in a line waiting for a clerk who was stationed behind a window. It looked like the customer was being punished. So I decided that I would personally take care of the adjustments.

To me, the litmus test of an adjustment on a return was what the customer felt in her mind was fair. We always tried to bend over backward to be fair.

Let's say a customer returns something that has been hanging in her closet for six months and has never been worn. What do you do? She's a good customer of ours and has never done anything like this before. You must evaluate each person and each situation. If she's had it for two years, then we don't think she should be returning it. On the other hand, if a husband comes in with his wife's unworn shoes (still in the boxes) after she has passed away, we take those shoes back because that's a sensitive time.

Now, if somebody goes too far, we'll say that although fairness is our credo and how we try to live our retail life, this adjustment is not fair. We're not afraid of saying that to a customer, but we don't say it very often. We're fond of saying to our people, "Let us tell the customer no. You say yes." The ones we say no to are people who have a lengthy history of wearing something and then returning it to us. We usually have their purchase history in front of us, so we can show them their past record. We'll say to that customer, "We can't be in business and provide good service if we keep taking back these types of returns. And we can't do it only for you because it's not fair to the other customers."

Sure, we occasionally get people mad at us. But interestingly enough, a lot of people get turned around and become fairly good customers. I've said to some customers, "That's it. You can't come into our store anymore." A week later, I get a call from them apologizing. I say, "Okay, but can you understand where we're coming from?"

When our generation started to run the business, it dawned on us that the more liberal we got with how we handled returns, the more business we did. We don't do this because we're good guys; we do it because it works. We want to do more business. It serves our purpose to be nice to people, to wait on them, to turn the other cheek. We've always believed that the happiest customer is the one leaving the store with a shopping bag in her hand.

Incidentally, our annual sales per square foot is one of the highest in the industry. The way we handle returns actually allows us to sell more merchandise. It drives traffic into our stores because customers trust that we stand behind the merchandise we sell. Though it's difficult to impossible to measure, it could be the most valuable aspect of our business.

ANSWER YOUR PHONE

Another way we are more accessible to the customer is by answering our own phone. I've taken thousands of calls over the years from customers who had one thing or another to say about how we were doing our business.

One day, I was in my office, my phone rang, and I answered it: "Hello."

Big silence. Then the voice on the other end said, "Is this Bruce Nordstrom?"

"Yes."

He introduced himself and then proceeded to explain that he was attending a Tom Peters seminar in Toronto. They were on a break. Before the break, Peters had told the audience he advocated that executives answer their own phones. But, he said, the only ones who do it are the Nordstroms.

This caller was so happy to find out this was true, he told Peters and the rest of the audience about it at the start of the next session in the seminar. It generated a big round of applause. Peters later sent me a thank-you note for validating what he had said.

In this world of automated phone systems, we still make sure that when somebody calls a Nordstrom store, the phone is answered by a human being.

Because our reputation is fragile, we must take care of every customer.

JIM NORDSTROM

Jim Nordstrom was a passionate supporter of the company's approach to handling returns. The following was taken from an interview he gave shortly before he passed away, in 1996.

All great companies that I know of became great by unconditionally guaranteeing everything they sold, with a smile. In his book, J. C. Penney wrote that when he was in Wyoming with his first store, the same lady would come in every year with her kid's underwear and say, "I'm not happy with it." He'd give her a whole new stack of underwear, no questions asked. But they were in his store. They weren't in the store across the street. He made a helluva living doing that.

Sam Walton used to say that if someone comes into your store unhappy and you make them happy, add 50 grand to the value of your company. If they walk out unhappy, subtract 100 grand. So, when you're fighting over a $9.95 item, you have to wonder what you are really doing in terms of the value of the company.

When Betsy Sanders opened our first store in California, her number one motto was "I don't want anyone in California to have anything in their home they bought at Nordstrom that they are unhappy with." I think she told that to every single salesperson in that store every day. She beat it into them. We were such a breath of fresh air down there. She made a lot of money for us, big time, with that policy.

Returns are the best way in the world for us to own the customer forever. When somebody comes in with a return, that's the time to really separate yourself from your competition. Greet them with a big smile. With the kind of prices that we charge, if people don't feel they can return an item if something's wrong with it, they aren't going to buy it. In the case of shoes, they may walk around forever to make sure they fit. If you take back the item with a smile and no questions asked and the customer walks out the door happy, what's that worth? That's worth a lot. It's the best sales closure we have as a company. If you have any problem, bring it back.

Returns are also the best way to control and improve quality. A buyer won't keep buying stuff that is of poor quality and gets returned. If we don't take it back, the buyer will continue to buy it. It doesn't hurt them. But if it comes back, they won't continue buying it.

Companies will always crack down on return policies. Salespeople get beat up and they get down in the dumps. But we have to continue to remind our people of the pluses of the return policy. You have to remember that the person who's returning that item is back in our store.

THE POSITIVES OF OUR RETURN POLICY

Mr. Jim's list of reasons for our return policy is still used today in our talks with our salespeople.

1. It is the principal reason why people walk in the door.

2. It's a lot easier to sell when people are confident that they can bring it back for any reason.

3. It improves our quality. Our buyers will insist on well-made garments from our vendors.

4. It improves our reputation for integrity.

5. What a wonderful opportunity for a salesperson to own a customer.

ARGUS

The Pacific Northwest's Independent Magazine of News, Comment and Opinion

Volume 81, No. 20   SEATTLE, Washington   May 17, 1974   25c

The Nordstrom Dynasty Is Still Going Strong

By DAVID BREWSTER

NEXT TUESDAY, at 11 a.m., stockholders of Nordstrom Inc. will gather for their annual meeting in the handsome top-floor suite of the company's elegant new downtown store. It ought to be a happy occasion, for several simple reasons:

● Last year, for the first time, Nordstrom topped $100-million in sales—a dramatic rise from sales figures of about $15-million 11 years ago, when the family-shoestore became a specialty fashion-chain. First-quarter sales are also up briskly for this year.

● This spring alone, Nordstrom has opened three new stores and expanded another. For EXPO, Nordstrom opened a 90,000-square-foot downtown Spokane store that is already a big hit; two weeks later a 70,000-square-foot store opened in Portland suburb Washington Square; Southcenter has added 20,000 square feet; Aurora Village gained a 60,000-square-foot Nordstrom. Making money in the suburbs is a pushover for the fashionable Nordstroms; unlike most retailers, Nordstrom is also able to do well downtown. The $9 million downtown-Seattle store is running 20 percent ahead of projected sales, already hitting 1977 figures. Having opened five new stores in the past two years, Nordstrom now has

The second-and third-generation Nordstroms, master-retailers of shoes and clothes. Top row: Jim, Bruce and Lloyd Nordstrom; bottom row: John and Elmer Nordstrom, Jack McMillan.
—sketch by mike casad

This sketch accompanied a 1974 article titled "The Nordstrom Dynasty Is Still Going Strong" in the Argus, *a local weekly publication.*

CHAPTER 14

A CHANGING OF THE GUARD

Everett, Elmer, and Lloyd had decided early on that, for the good of the company, each of them would retire when he reached age 65. As Elmer wrote in his book:

Too often, we saw businesses fail because they were run by an older family member who refused to relinquish his position. Many times as the founder of a business grows old, his thinking becomes more inclined toward security, and risks are avoided that might have led to growth. Employees won't find much incentive for coming up with new ideas if they know they'll be viewed as too risky by an older, conservative boss. The result is sometimes an old taskmaster, surrounded by "Yes-Men," rather than people who want to take charge and produce.

My grandfather retired at 58 to give his sons their chance. As my father and uncles were heading toward age 65, they began to think about doing the same. My father turned 65 in 1968. Elmer would reach that age in 1969, and Lloyd in 1975.

One day, after Everett and Elmer had retired, they (along with Lloyd) called John, Jim, Jack, and me into their office and told us that it was dawning on them that they didn't have much in the way of retirement savings. They each owned a third of the company. At the time, we were a private company that didn't declare dividends because they had always wanted to use that money for expansion. The three drew the same salary every year, and after they retired, they would no longer draw income from the company.

Lloyd had three daughters (Loyal, who was married to Jack McMillan; Linda; and Susan), who were not involved in the business. Elmer's kids, John and Jim, were both in the business. In my dad's case, there was me and my sister, Anne, who was married with kids.

My generation had a chance to take it even further, to become a national company, and to leave it better than we found it.

The brothers needed an estate for their children who did not participate in the company, so they had to find a way to generate some liquidity. They told John, Jim, Jack, and me that there were three options:

(1) We could buy them out, which is what they had done with their father. That was not feasible. Although the company could have borrowed the money, the debt would have strapped us for 15 years, and we wouldn't have been able to grow the business. Of course, when they bought the business from my grandpa, it was in the form of an IOU, and they gradually paid him back.

(2) They could sell out to another company. At the time, we weren't sure how many other retailers would be interested in us, but we soon discovered that several companies were. We were a little company that all of a sudden was on the move, just becoming visible.

(3) We could take the company public. That was not anybody's first choice.

Among the most prominent potential suitors were Macy's, Associated Dry Goods, and Dayton-Hudson Corporation. But the principal suitor was Broadway-Hale (which was later called Carter Hawley Hale, then Broadway Stores).

Ed Carter, chairman of Broadway-Hale, came up with the most money. It involved a million shares of stock in Broadway-Hale, valued at about $24 a share. In those days, the investment community categorized the value of individual companies' stocks by "tiers." Larger, older companies were given top-tier status and were rewarded with a price–earnings ratio higher than that of smaller, newer companies. We were doing about $40 million a year in sales, which gave us third-tier status.

The closer we got to the deal, the more convinced my cousins and I were that we didn't want to work for those guys. We saw all their problems. We had visited their stores and they didn't look very good to us, and we thought their service was uniformly bad. In most cases, their real estate was a combination of good locations and very old, broken-down locations in areas that they shouldn't have been in.

The possibility of working for someone else was a catalyst for us to come up with an alternative game plan that would make sense to the three brothers. Our driving stimulus was the realization that we had a chance to do something pretty big. Our grandpa got credit for starting the company. His three sons built it into a very viable business. My generation had a chance to take it even further, to become a national company, and to leave it better than we found it — just as the previous generation had done.

By the time we made our presentation to Everett, Elmer, and Lloyd, we had our plan down on paper. It wasn't a work of art; we did it with our guts and our brains. (More guts than brains; we felt it more than we understood it.) We had our projections and where we thought we could go, and we described how fast we could grow this company geographically. We had been in the apparel business for a few years and were doing well, and it seemed to us that there was a huge retailing hole we could fill. We thought we had an advantage over other retailers in terms of customer service.

God bless Everett, Elmer, and Lloyd because they agreed to do it. If personal greed had been the main factor, they would have gone with Broadway-Hale.

I think what ultimately sold them was that we were unanimous in our approach. We came to them as a group and presented our game plan. They realized how hard we were working, and I think they liked the fact that we were putting ourselves on the line, with the full understanding that we had our work cut out for us.

After they agreed, we thought, "Oh, my God. We got what we asked for." That was scary.

When my dad and uncles told Mr. Carter of their decision, he immediately flew to Seattle to try to change their minds. While he was here, I met with Mr. Carter and told him that he was the guy we were down to, "but we want it to be our own company." He told me that we would be the biggest shareholders in Broadway-Hale and that we would be running it. That prospect didn't excite us. Finally, he said, "You're making a huge mistake."

I'm not smart, but I am competitive. I said, "Why do you say that?"

He said, "The value of the Nordstrom company will never be recognized at the level that I am recognizing it today with this offer."

Three years later, the value of our company would be much higher than what he thought we were worth. Today, of course, Broadway-Hale is no longer in business.

GOING PUBLIC

The only way to pay our fathers for the business would be to raise money by selling stock through an initial public offering. The company wouldn't be able to pay dividends at first, but Everett, Elmer, and Lloyd would have something of value (stock shares) that they could sell or pass on to their heirs.

My dad and my uncles just didn't like the idea of becoming a public company and having to show their numbers to everybody. Not only that, but my dad said, "We live in Seattle, where everybody's our friend, and many of them will buy our stock. What happens when the price of the stock goes down?" They didn't relish the idea of walking around Seattle and running into friends who had lost money on Nordstrom stock.

Although we would have preferred not to publicly air our financial situation, all of us (including the brothers) knew that we were ready to bust out. John, Jim, Jack, and I were young and full of beans. The company had made the leap into the apparel business, and we had made the leap into other geographic regions. In order for this company to really grow, we needed the availability of funds.

My dad was the first of the three brothers to say, "Let's go public. It's the third generation's business now." The brothers were going to be the biggest shareholders, but our generation would be running the business.

The brothers were not reluctant to take chances; they gambled a lot in the shoe stores by buying fashion on the come. If we thought something was going to be really big the next season, we would make a big order, rather than take a dibs-and-dabs approach. When there was shoe rationing during the Second World War, the brothers prepaid bills, which was a calculated gamble. So was going public. God bless them, they said, "We're going to do it even though we don't like the sound of it."

Our initial public offering was issued in July 1971, with Goldman, Sachs & Co. and Blyth & Co. as our original two investment bankers. The

The cover of our first annual shareholders report, in 1971

No question about it, we were a growth stock.

investment public saw us as a burgeoning small company that could fill a niche in the market and had great growth potential. No question about it, we were a growth stock.

It was my job to speak to the analysts. Allan Goesling, who was our chief financial officer, put together some charts and graphs that measured our growth and illustrated where we saw our opportunities. It was similar to what we had done to help sell our fathers on the deal.

For our first analysts' meeting, we rented a hotel meeting room in New York. As I stood at the podium with my slides, I began to get a little nervous. About 10 minutes before we were about to start, there was nobody in the room, and I began to think that no one cared. But with about five minutes to go, people started coming in, which made me even more nervous.

I was reminded of a speech class I took as a freshman in college. We would be assigned a topic and have to give an impromptu speech. Those speeches would kill me. I would suffer and shake, and my voice would quaver, and I would earn one of my usual C's. Now here I was at this hotel in New York, ready to talk about a topic I actually knew a lot about. Still, I was very nervous.

As the room filled up, I looked at all these analysts and saw that they were in their thirties, just like me! It turned out that investment banking firms would send their junior people to these due diligence meetings, so it was on the record that people from Goldman Sachs, Merrill Lynch, etc., were there. Well, heck, they knew less than I did! Once I realized that, I loosened up and was able to give my presentation with some confidence.

My pitch was that our point of difference, which was going to allow this company to grow and be successful, was that we take care of the customer. To most analysts, customer service sounded like a throwaway line, but to us, the best service you can give is to sell something.

I told analysts that we were different from other retailers because we had better people. By that I didn't mean that our people were smarter or more experienced than our competitors'. What I meant was that our people performed better than those of our competitors, and that the

Myself with Lloyd, Elmer, and John outside the Bellevue store in 1967

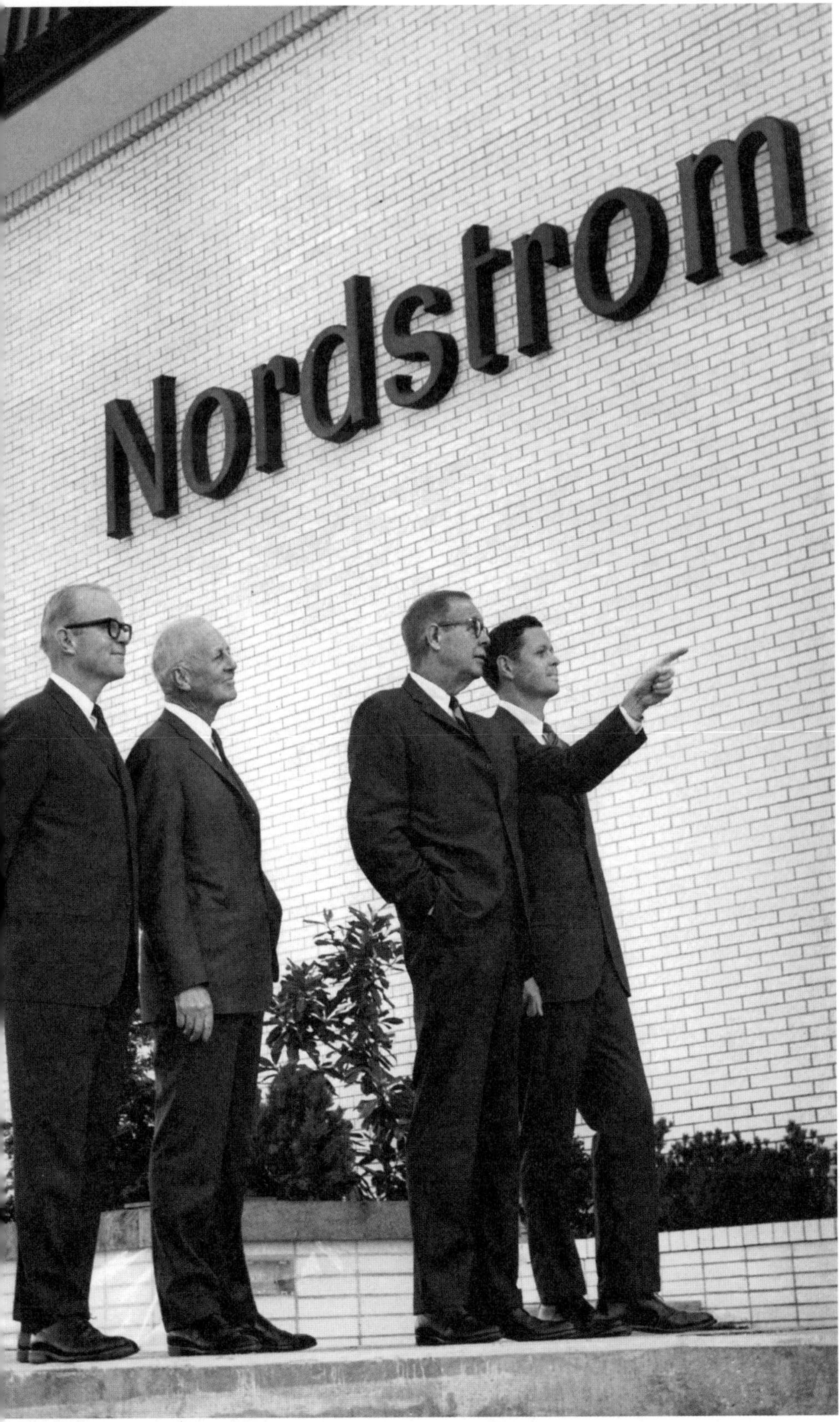
Nordstrom

most important decisions affecting the company were made as close as possible to the customer.

A few years after we went public, we were doing fine, so I decided I wasn't going to worry about analysts or curry favor with them. In those days, when the security laws were less stringent, you could have individual conversations with analysts. You can still have those individual conversations today, but with the impact of the Sarbanes-Oxley Act (officially known as the Public Company Accounting Reform and Investor Protection Act of 2002), you must be absolutely sure that — in the interest of full disclosure — everybody is given all the same pertinent information at exactly the same time.

At one point, I was scheduled for an appointment with a D. DeMoss, an analyst from Dean Witter. I didn't know that the D stood for Donna. Through the door of my office came an attractive young blond woman, the first female analyst I ever knew. (Remember, we're talking about the early 1970s.) As I began to give her my spiel, she stopped me and said, "I know what you're up to. For the last three days I've been in Seattle, and I've shopped your downtown store and all your suburban stores. You give better service than everyone else."

She saw what we were doing, not only through her intellect but also through her experience as a shopper. Although she lived in New York and shopped all the big stores, she said, "I'd rather buy clothes and shoes here than in New York."

Most analysts don't want to talk about the shopping experience; they want to talk about numbers and ratios. But she got it. She was one of the

To most analysts, customer service sounded like a throwaway line, but to us, the best service you can give is to sell something.

first analysts who came out with an enthusiastic report on us. Two other analysts who really got our deal early on were Joe Ellis and Maggie Gilliam. They also understood our customer orientation and how that set us apart from our competitors and created value. After that, others started jumping on the bandwagon.

THE GOESLINGS: FATHER AND SON

One of the most fortunate aspects of our growth as a company was the fact that for almost half a century, we had just two chief financial officers, Allan Goesling and his son, John Goesling. Both father and son were excellent CPAs, and were uniquely well suited to Nordstrom because they truly understood the fact that nothing happens in our company until someone sells something. Most financial types lose sight of that simple truth somewhere along the line.

When Allan Goesling retired in 1980, it was my job to find a successor. I despaired of doing so until we realized that we had someone in-house who was well prepared for the job: Allan's son John. He had come to work for us in 1977 and before that had worked for our company as a stockboy when he was in high school, so he understood the Nordstrom culture and was in a position to hit the ground running.

INVERTED PYRAMID

Our inverted-pyramid structure has become one of the best-known elements of our company. Its origins date back to the days before we went public. Preparing for a due diligence meeting with analysts in New York, we were told that we had to show them our company's organizational chart. We laughed about the fact that we'd never had an organizational chart, but in thinking about it, we began to realize that the best way to illustrate what we actually do was to take the standard organizational pyramid and turn it on its head: the inverted pyramid was born! I believe John actually came up with that. As the accompanying illustration shows, the inverted pyramid places our salespeople at the top, closest to our customers.

Initially, it didn't go over all that well with analysts, who thought it was simplistic at best. Eventually, though, as people got to know our

customers

sales and support people

department managers

buyers • merchandise managers
store managers • regional managers

executive team
board of directors

Our company's organizational chart, the inverted pyramid, illustrates our belief that the most important people in our company are our salespeople, as they are closest to our customers.

company, they changed their minds, and they came to understand that the inverted pyramid sets us apart from other retailers.

Obviously, as we've grown into an $8 billion company, and as we've had to add more layers of management, the organizational chart has been tweaked and changed. But the philosophy behind the pyramid remains intact.

Empowering our people goes hand in hand with the inverted pyramid. We believe in empowering people as close to the customer as we can, in order for those people to bring an entrepreneurial, proprietary attitude to their business. You have to be confident enough in your system and your people to take your hands off and allow the business to work. Everett, Elmer, and Lloyd taught us that, by giving managers the freedom to run their departments, they got the very best performance. Managers have to be empowered and respected and know that it's their call, and their reputation. Most of our competitors' stores are faceless; you go into a department and you notice that there is not one person who is obviously in charge, taking ownership.

When it came to emphasizing empowerment, there was no blinding flash of insight. The idea evolved over time, and the more we did it, the better our performance. The same thing with our approach to returns: the more liberal we got, the better we did.

In our one-page employee handbook, our one rule is "Use good judgment in all situations." Jim came up with that one. What a terrific idea! We're all accustomed to seeing voluminous employee handbooks that are strict and narrow. We made ours as simple as possible. Today, with the labor laws being what they are, you have to provide lots of other employee information, but when it comes to taking care of the customer at Nordstrom, there is still only one rule.

SHARING THE POWER

One of the things that my dad and uncles were concerned about was who was going to be the boss among those of us in the third generation. Originally, I was the president, but one day my cousin John, who is three years younger than I am, came to me and said, "I don't know if I want to work for you my whole life."

I said, "I respect that 100 percent. I don't want to be your boss for your whole life."

I talked to Lloyd, my dad, and Elmer, and told them, "As far as I'm concerned, these guys want us all to be equal, and I'm on their side." The company was considerably bigger and there was plenty to do, and the more I thought about it, the more enthusiastic I became. While

Managers have to be empowered and respected and know that it's their call, and their reputation.

the brothers had their reservations about this arrangement, I had none because I was confident that we could be successful. My best argument was "We want to do it the way you did."

Although Lloyd played devil's advocate, there was not a serious fight. The brothers liked the fact that we had resolved this issue ourselves. We created an Office of the President, making us co-presidents, with different responsibilities. We didn't get penalized by the financial community for having four co-presidents, and I don't think it mattered one way or the other because even before we became co-presidents, we had already divided the business responsibilities among ourselves.

Shoes were still by far the biggest part of the business. Initially, I headed up women's shoes, John headed up men's apparel and shoes, Jack had women's ready-to-wear, and Jim oversaw juniors, sportswear, and children's shoes. John was always interested in the operations, as was his father, Elmer. Jim took advertising and PR. Jack took over budgeting, setting goals for expense control, and reviewing the monthly P&L statement. I took investor relations and Wall Street, and the chief financial officer was my direct report.

Obviously, the arrangement worked out great. It was marvelous for them and it was marvelous for me because it felt like a weight had been taken off my shoulders. We knew pretty darn quickly that things were working because we were clicking off big increases, and we started getting it to the bottom line, which we had not previously been famous for doing.

In the early 1970s, some analysts tried to pigeonhole us somewhere in between the moderate Joseph Magnin chain and the better I. Magnin chain. Although we had some things in common with both extremes, we felt that, being from the Pacific Northwest, we needed to cover a much broader spectrum than either of those stores. Frankly, the store that we looked up to the most, and tried to emulate in many respects, was Saks Fifth Avenue, which we considered the kings of the specialty store operators.

Obviously, the arrangement worked out great. It was marvelous for them and it was marvelous for me because it felt like a weight had been taken off my shoulders.

DEVELOPING THE MEN'S BUSINESS

By the time we got into men's apparel, it was easier for us to gain acceptance in the industry because we had already achieved some size and credibility through our success in selling women's apparel.

The men's business was my cousin John's baby. While we wanted to be as fashionable as we could in the women's business, John's approach in men's was to make it traditional, which was the predominant business style of the day. He was a natural-shoulder, button-down shirt, cuffs-on-the-pants guy, and that's what most men wanted. When trendy men's fashions such as Nehru jackets and polyester suits reared their ugly heads, John said no. Countless men bought those items, which would hang in their closets and never be worn, reminding them every day of their mistake. They didn't buy them at Nordstrom. We ended up owning the traditional men's business, which saw dramatic growth.

John Nordstrom stands in the new men's sportswear department of our Bellevue store, 1967.

John selected and worked with Jack Irving, who was the corporate merchandise manager of our men's business. Jack proved to be one of the best merchants we ever had. He and John made a wonderful team, and they set a great standard for all of us.

In recent years, the whole men's tailored-clothing industry has been in the doldrums, and we have had to change our approach to the business, which is terrific now. I think John would say it would be more terrific if we had stuck to the original idea.

CONFRONTING OUR FIRST CHALLENGES

It wasn't long after we took over that we faced our first challenge: the famous "Boeing Bust" of the early 1970s. Responding to a national aerospace recession, Boeing, the city's biggest employer, slashed its workforce from 80,400 to 37,200 people, and suddenly Seattle had 13.8 percent unemployment. Many people left the city for greener pastures. Things were so bad that somebody put up a billboard that read: "Will the last person leaving Seattle turn out the lights."

As dark as that period was, we were inspired to be bold and aggressive. We took a page from our fathers' playbook. During World War II, when shoes were being rationed and other retailers were cutting back, they forged ahead, and grew their business. We saw the Boeing downturn as a similar opportunity for us because other retailers were pulling in their horns, buying less inventory, and running fewer newspaper advertisements. We didn't believe the gloom and doom in the media; we only believed in our sales numbers and our gut. Our goal was to make our numbers and we did, not by buying less merchandise and firing more employees, but by outworking the competition. We were still just a Northwest company, so all of us Nordstroms could be in the stores a lot, talking to our people and keeping up their spirits. Our company's morale stayed surprisingly good, considering all the negative things that were going on. That one year, 1971, was probably the best we ever had because although we saw only a modest 4 percent increase, we dramatically improved our share of the market, even though it was a smaller market.

All this was happening around the time we were going public. We'd had this grand scheme of taking off like a rocket, but then all of a sudden we were faced with this downturn in our home base. That made our game plan a little scarier, but it didn't dissuade us at all. We worked harder, and we came out of it in better shape.

In 1973, despite the continued downturn in the Seattle market, we demonstrated our faith in our hometown by expanding our downtown store, uniting the adjoining Ranke, Gottstein, and Best's buildings into one big store. We budgeted $6 million and ended up spending $11 million (a lot of money for us in those days) on the expansion. At the store opening in November, I was quoted in the *Seattle Post-Intelligencer:* "We can build suburban stores forever and they will be successful. But this — by a mile — is the biggest thing we ever did."

With the opening of the newly renovated downtown store, we officially changed the name of the company from Nordstrom Best to Nordstrom because we felt that the Nordstrom name had been established in the apparel industry. The name change also made it simpler for customers and for store logistics.

In 1973, our sales exceeded $100 million for the first time. That year, we were operating 11 stores and 32 leased shoe departments. Only five years earlier, we'd had sales of $40 million. Two years later, in 1975, we opened the first Nordstrom Rack in the lower level of the new store as a clearance center for full-line merchandise.

DECISION BY COMMITTEE

John, Jim, Jack, and I developed a respectful camaraderie. We didn't see each other socially very much and we were very different people, but we all had mutual respect for what the other guy brought to the table. That became very clear whenever we had disagreements, and there were a lot of disagreements, as there should be. That's the beauty of a committee, as far as I'm concerned. How we arrived at conclusions and solutions gave us a lot of confidence that we could go further.

Jim had a unique way of getting to the heart of the matter. He had an unusually sensitive feeling for most of the issues of the day and was able to identify the right direction to take, often in a humorous fashion.

Jim also had an instinct for retailing and was the best salesman of the four of us. I'll never forget the first day he began selling in the basement of Rhodes, when he was still a teenager. Around noon, I decided to go down to the basement to get Jim and take him to lunch. But when I got there, he was gone. One of his co-workers said, "Jim left a long time ago." He left? He'd just started, and it was only noon. Turns out, his very first customer was a lady from an orphanage who was buying shoes for all the girls. She had a list of sizes she had to buy in this one style of shoe, which Jim sold to her. He made his draw for the day, so he figured he could go home. That was Jim. He was the most fun-loving and easygoing of the four of us.

John, Jim, and I could not have been more fortunate than to have Jack as a part of our team. Jack, who became a relative when he married our cousin Loyal, didn't start out in this business as a kid (as had my cousins and I), but once he joined our company, he was eager, willing, and able to do all the hands-on, nitty-gritty things that needed to be done. Jack truly understood our way of doing things and the culture that has made Nordstrom unique. He was usually a calming influence in our meetings and would help to keep us on the right track. One of Jack's favorite tasks was educating our employees about setting goals. He also looked for ways to improve the incentives we offered our teams for reaching goals. He is a spiritual man whose deep-rooted faith and desire to connect with people led him to become very active in our community, supporting disadvantaged people. Jack's contributions have made a lasting impact on the reputation of our company.

Brothers Jim and John Nordstrom were different from their dad and different from each other, which worked well for us. When we discussed things, and disagreed, there were often two sides presented very vociferously by the two of them. Then we'd vote, and if you were on the losing side, you didn't hang your head. The attitude was, okay, if that's what we're going to do, then we're going to do it all out.

Our dads set a great example for us. They'd go into a meeting, shut the door, and always come out of that meeting of one mind. That's what we wanted to do.

To understand the dynamics of our committee, you have to know that we started with the unanimous feeling that we wanted to be of one mind. This didn't mean that we wouldn't disagree with one another. That was the strength of our setup — we all had the same goal, but we had different ideas about how to reach that goal. I think that if you've got the right people, you'll come out with the right answer more often than not.

As a practical matter, John tended to be the black hat. Jim, Jack, and I wanted to seize most growth opportunities. Because John would play devil's advocate and ask the most probing questions, it compelled us to present the facts that would support our position. Once John was satisfied, he became as enthusiastic as the rest of us. John gets all the credit in the world because the minute that decision was set, then he almost became the leader of it. His philosophy was: If we're going to do this, we're going to do this as one.

For example, as we went along, we acquired a few little businesses that didn't work out. For several years, we sold shoes in a store called Adams in Bellingham and at Lou Johnson's in Tacoma. When expansion opportunities for our larger stores were not available, we responded by establishing a new store division called Place Two, which featured younger merchandise, both apparel and shoes, in stores that were 17,000 to 30,000 square feet. Primarily located in smaller communities in Washington, Oregon, and Montana, our 11 Place Two stores allowed us to keep our company growing, albeit with a different store format. As it turned out, those stores did not deliver the same kind of sales per square foot and profitability figures that we were able to generate in our larger stores, and we eventually divested ourselves of them, rather than continuing to knock our heads against the wall. We have discovered over the years that our stores do best in areas with large populations, and when we can give customers a complete offering. We don't want to disappoint customers.

But other than that, I think we made good decisions in sticking to our knitting. I can't think of anything we were looking at doing in a relatively major way that we backed off and then later said, thank God we didn't do that.

MY FATHER PASSES AWAY

All of this success was tempered by the loss of my father. Learning about his passing is a horrible memory of mine.

On July 1, 1972, a beautiful Saturday afternoon, I left work early to spend the weekend with my family at our cabin up on Whidbey Island. To get to Whidbey, you have to catch the ferry at Mukilteo. I drove onto the ferry and turned on my car radio as we made the short trip to Whidbey. Listening to the news, I suddenly heard: "One of Seattle's finest businessmen, Everett Nordstrom, just died."

The news floored me. My dad had been playing golf that day, and died of a heart attack halfway through the 17th hole, going uphill. Although there was a group of physicians on the course at the time, they couldn't revive him.

When we landed at Whidbey, I drove to the cabin and told Fran what had happened. I then turned around and went back home to find my mother.

Most people who die are generally either sick or real old or both. You have time to come to grips with it, but we didn't have that with my dad, whom I considered indestructible. He was only 69, very healthy, and took such good care of himself. To hear the news on the radio was pretty cold.

In an editorial in the *Seattle Times*, they wrote, "A remarkable team of brothers who have provided civic and business leadership to this community for a number of decades was broken up by death this past weekend. . . . Everett Nordstrom will be greatly missed in the community in which he lived and worked throughout his life."

I couldn't have said it better myself.

SOME VERY SPECIAL SPOUSES

I'd like to say a few words about the spouses in our generation. Interestingly, the wives of John and Jim are both named Sally. To avoid confusion, they are known in our family as Sally A and Sally B, or Blonde Sally (John's wife) and Dark Sally (Jim's wife). John's Sally, besides helping to raise three extraordinary children (Jim, John E., and Kristie) and being the proud grandmother of 11 grandchildren, has been involved in a wide variety of civic and philanthropic endeavors, and is most proficient at growing roses. Jim's Sally raised four terrific children (Dan, Bill, Charlie, and Jamie) and has nine grandchildren, and is also very giving of herself for civic causes. Both Sallys have excellent taste, and their respective homes are truly very special places to visit.

Jack was married to Lloyd's oldest daughter, my dear cousin Loyal, and they are the parents of five marvelous children (Keri, Laurie, John, David, and Wendy), and four grandchildren. Sadly, they divorced. Jack is now married to an energetic lady named Alex, who is a joy to be around.

THE ROLE OF WOMEN

In the old days, there were few women shoe salespeople in our industry, and Nordstrom, like our competitors, was probably 90 percent male. The women who survived and thrived in a male-dominated system were tough because they had to be. They worked primarily in children's shoes, handbags, and the office. As for Nordstrom family members, the only two women who worked for us in a significant way were my sister, Anne, who performed so well in many jobs before she married and had kids, and now is our corporate contributions director; and John's daughter, Kristie, who did a great job for us in HR in Southern California. Then she got married, had kids, and didn't want to work outside the home. Lloyd's three daughters, who all married and had families, had no interest in working for the company. To the best of my knowledge, there are no frustrated women in our family who wanted to be a part of this company and weren't given the opportunity.

As we grew and got more into fashion, it dawned on us that it was in our best interest to hire and promote women as buyers and merchandise managers. We put together an incredibly talented and driven group of women who helped to make this company what it is today, among them Betsy Sanders, Dale Cameron, Sue Patneaude, Gail Cottle, Cindy Paur, Sue Tabor, Jammie Baugh, Galen Jefferson, Linda Finn, and Susan Brotman, who are a group of great role models and mentors for all the people — women and men — in our company.

Today, our workforce is about 70 percent women; 71 percent of our managers are women, and we are considered one of the best companies in America for women.

We put together an incredibly talented and driven group of women who helped to make this company what it is today.

GAIL COTTLE

Gail joined our company in May 1969, at the age of 17, when she was hired by her neighbor Adolph Frank, who was managing our shoe store in Yakima. She retired in 2002 as an executive vice president.

In our company, learning how to sell shoes was the precursor for learning how to sell every idea, every plan, everything that required a vote from management. You had to present your merchandise, make your case, make sure it fit the parameters, and then close the sale.

The Nordstroms empowered people with a challenge. They asked enough questions to make you go back and look at your plan again. Once they said they were with you, they let you run your business and play it out. That's a wonderful feeling because you're always going to have a hiccup.

For example, when I became corporate merchandise manager for juniors, the business had not been good. I wanted to create a new in-store environment, and worked very closely with Bud Erickson and our interior designer. After doing a lot of research, I decided on an open warehouse with weird lights, and TV monitors with music videos, which was a radical departure from what any major retailer had ever done.

I presented this idea at a store planning meeting, where you had to get the stamp of approval from Bruce, John, Jim, Jack, and Bob Bender. I remember the looks on their faces. None of them said very much. Bruce's arms were folded, which was not a good sign. Finally, he smiled and said, "Okay, Gail, we're with you on a win, and we'll be with you on a draw."

The message was clear: This is a big change and a big expense. We're going to go with you on it, but it had better be good.

Of course, that made you work your fanny off, like there was no tomorrow. But it worked. It helped turn around our juniors business.

John began working part-time for the company when he was 15 and continued while he was in college. After working at the Arthur Andersen accounting firm, he joined Nordstrom in 1977, and three years later succeeded his father as CFO.

I wasn't necessarily Bruce's first choice to replace my father. He had three years of seeing what I could do, but I hadn't had any CFO experience and I was pretty green. He talked to a few other people, and when he eventually offered me the job, I was overwhelmed.

That whole hiring process reflects a characteristic of Bruce that he used a lot in his business dealings. He was not necessarily interested in your pedigree; he was more interested in your character and what kind of person you were. Obviously, he could have found people with more credentials than I had at that time.

In many companies, the CFO gets a lot of pressure from the bosses to make sure the numbers come out right, so that they meet Wall Street's expectations. I can't remember a single instance of Mr. Bruce saying to me, "I don't like the results you came up with; go back and fix it." His integrity was unquestioned.

As a result, as we look back over the period when my father and I were CFOs, we never had a major accounting problem or issue. That's a tribute to the upper management of the company.

On a more humorous note, I remember the time a customer returned a purchase to the store and received a credit. Somehow, the credit was one penny less than what she had paid for the merchandise. She wrote a letter to Mr. Bruce complaining about it. Mr. Bruce wrote back to her, apologizing for the error, and pasted a penny to the bottom of the letter.

Cindy Paur joined Nordstrom in 1968, and became the youngest person and the second woman to be named a company vice president. She led the marketing division for 15 years and was a member of the Executive Committee before retiring in 1996.

When I think of Jim, I think back more than 30 years ago when the Nordstrom family was trying to decide which of them was going to manage the women's apparel side of the business. Jim, John, Bruce, and Jack were all shoe dogs, so shoes were where they were most comfortable. Jim volunteered to take the women's business, where most of the merchandising jobs were filled by women.

This was a pivotal time for women in the workforce in general, and at Nordstrom in particular. The women who were working for the company back then knew that if you wanted to be taken seriously, and if you wanted to have a management position, you were going to have to prove yourself.

Jim had an incredible sensitivity to the employees and had the ability to impart empowerment. When you met with him, he made you feel that you were his most important merchant. But 10 minutes later, the next merchant he spoke to felt the very same way. He had the ability to make you believe that you could accomplish anything. He did not over-manage. I made zillions of mistakes that he probably could have kept me from, but I learned a lot from those mistakes. All of the fellows were good at that, which was their management style.

Jim had his father's sense of humor. He was a magnet for people. He was the most verbally passionate about our customer service.

Back in the 1980s, when we were all trying to sort out the role of women in the workplace, we had a couple of women in management who were pregnant. I asked Mr. Jim how I should handle that. He looked at me, in typical Mr. Jim management fashion, and said, "I was talking to the other guys about this over coffee. We don't know. We think it's great that you're in a spot to make that decision because you're a woman. Whatever you think is great with us. It's up to you."

Susan came to Nordstrom in 1973, and ultimately became a member of our Executive Committee. She left the company in 1979 to start a family.

After working as a buyer, I was named sales promotion manager, which was an unlikely move, and I was terrified. But it was very typical of the way Nordstrom operated — they gave people the opportunity to go beyond their training, and beyond what they felt was their capacity.

Nordstrom was a particularly good place for young women. There was a sense that there were no boundaries, that you could go as far as your ability would take you. We knew that there would be something on the horizon, and usually in a very short period. If you worked hard and did a good job, you knew that you would be rewarded with a new job and a promotion of some kind. Often, it wasn't something that any of us had anticipated. That was certainly the case when I became sales promotion director.

While other companies had formal training programs, Nordstrom just put us all out there to sink or swim. There was a sense of working together as a family toward the same goals.

We saw the family come in to work in the morning and leave at night. We knew they were watchful. We knew they cared about the people working there, and what kind of business they were doing day in and day out. We wanted to succeed as part of their team.

There was a meeting every Monday morning, which included Bruce, Jim, John, Jack, and Bob Bender, and the chief financial officer. Those meetings gave me an opportunity to watch them work and to see how they discussed every issue together and came to a decision. They made certain that they agreed on the decision before executing it. There was such respect among them that if someone felt strongly one way or another, they would talk it through until they arrived at what they felt was the best decision for the company.

CHAPTER 15

CALIFORNIA DREAMING

Throughout the 1970s, we grew steadily, with net sales reaching $128.7 million in 1975. Although we were still only in the Pacific Northwest, we believed we could take our model national. We didn't know how many stores we would have, but we realized that they had to be in relatively big cities.

It was obvious that to grow this business, California was where we had to go next. Thinking in purely geographic terms, we figured the logical first place would be San Francisco.

But then we got a visit from Henry Segerstrom, who owned and had developed the South Coast Plaza mall in Costa Mesa, California, in Orange County. He stopped by my office in Seattle and we began our discussions, which continued for a few years.

Henry's family history was remarkably similar to ours. His grandfather, C.J., left Sweden in 1882 — five years before my grandpa did the same thing. The Segerstrom family acquired 20 acres of Orange County land in 1898, and by the 1950s had turned it into 20,000 acres of lima bean fields, helping to make Costa Mesa the lima bean capital of the world. By the 1960s, Orange County was getting built up, and with the new San Diego (I-405) Freeway cutting through the bean fields, Henry saw the future. He and his family moved from lima beans to retail, resulting in the construction in 1967 of South Coast Plaza, one of the best shopping centers in the world.

It was shortly after South Coast opened that Henry came to Seattle to talk to my cousins and me about opening a store there. He told us he had visited a couple of our stores, particularly our downtown store,

We were betting everything we had on the move to South Coast.

Presenting our plans for expansion in California

and saw that we were different from the average retail operation. His bottom line was: "I'm always on the lookout for something that's different because malls are all starting to look the same. The stores are the same; the merchandise is the same."

If Henry hadn't approached us, we would never have thought of going directly to Southern California, which seemed to us like another world. To leapfrog all other possibilities, to go right to the number one shopping center — which was already anchored by Bullock's, May, Joseph Magnin, and Sears — was a major challenge. In addition to all that, Henry's terms were extremely tough, and building a store down there was going to be a major expense.

In 1975, we agreed to build the South Coast Plaza store.

One of our first questions was: Who is going to manage this store? The job would entail not just managing the store — a big task in and of itself — but also carrying our culture and our way of doing business to a place far away from Seattle.

Our first choice for the job was Bob Weil, a Yale graduate with an impressive academic background, who was one of the truly smart people in our company. We had inherited Bob from Best's Apparel; in fact, he was one of the few Best's employees who succeeded with us, winning the John W. Nordstrom Award in 1972. He was an earnest, honest, focused guy who understood what we were all about, and we thought he'd be perfect for the task. But in late 1977, about six months before we were going to open the store, Bob told us that he couldn't go to California because his wife didn't want to move.

We understood, and we supported his priorities. End of discussion. Then John, Jim, Jack, and I looked at each other and asked ourselves, "What do we do now?" We were betting everything we had on the move to South Coast. We wrote down on a sheet of paper the names of all the high-ranking people in our company, and then rated them: Who was the best storekeeper? The best merchant? The best expense person?

The answer to all of those questions was the same person: Betsy Sanders.

Betsy Sanders at the South Coast Plaza store

BETSY SANDERS

Let's go back to September 1971. I was sitting in my office at Best's Apparel, trying to learn the apparel business. It was the end of a difficult day, I was feeling grumpy, and my secretary came in and said, "There's a young woman named Betsy Sanders to see you."

I said, "Who is she?"

My secretary said her brother-in-law had recommended that she see me. I then remembered that about six months earlier, I had received a letter from a friend of mine who was an executive at the Brown Shoe Company. He wrote that his sister-in-law was moving to Seattle and asked if I would interview her for a job. I said sure, and immediately forgot about it.

In walked this 26-year-old woman, no makeup, not fashion-forward. She handed me her résumé, and I saw that she had all this high-level schooling, culminating at the University of Munich. Most recently, she had been a German teacher. I handed her résumé back to her and said, "Let's not go any further. You don't want to work for us."

She said, "What do you mean?"

I said, "The University of Munich? No one of that caliber has ever worked in this company. This is a tough, dirty business. Six days a week. Open at night. People yell at you. You would be much better off working in a law office five days a week, eight hours a day, with people that are more on your level, which is a higher level than we are."

She said, "I think I can do anything that you tell me to do."

Oh yeah, I thought. We'll see about that.

I picked up the phone and called our Northgate store manager, Jim Nicholson, who was then a star in our company. I said, "Jim, I never do this. But I have a young woman here that I want you to hire." In those days, we had a moderate-priced dress department called Miss Seattle Dresses, where the big line was Leslie Fay. I asked Jim to put Betsy in there and told her to report for work the next day.

A month or so later, I was talking to Jim Nicholson, and I asked him, "Whatever happened to that girl I sent out to you?"

He said she was the number one salesperson in her department. From what I knew about the department, the women who worked there were tough cookies who would not make it easy for an inexperienced youngster to survive. She was number one in that department? Wasn't I smart?

Four months later, Betsy became an assistant manager, and soon after that, a department manager. You just couldn't hold her back. People who worked with her couldn't begrudge her success because she was just that good. She was married and had two little kids, and she was very devoted to our business.

Eventually, she became store manager at Bellevue Square, and she excelled there as well. Her rise through the business world came at a time when the women's movement was just getting started. There weren't a lot of high-ranking females in companies. She went right to the top of our business.

What made Betsy so good? Simple. Betsy got it. She was a better Nordstrom than I was. She really understood what it meant to worship the customer, and she knew that nothing was ever going to happen around here until we sold something. Her numbers were always at the top of the list.

So when it came to deciding who was going to manage South Coast Plaza, Betsy was the leader in all the criteria. Of course, being the chauvinists that we were, we thought she wouldn't want to make the move. Her husband, Sandy, had a big sales job in Seattle with IBM. They had two houses; they had just bought a new one and were still trying to sell their old one. Finally, I said that we should at least tell her she was number one on our list, as a compliment to her stellar job performance.

I called her in the next morning and told her about South Coast Plaza. Her only question was: Is that an advancement? I said not initially, because Bellevue Square will do more business in that first year than South Coast Plaza. But if it does what we think it will do, the manager of that store will eventually run the biggest single part of this business.

She said, "I'd like to do that."

I said, "How about your kids and your husband?"

She said, "We've already had that discussion." Her husband, Sandy, had told her that he knew she was a heart-and-soul Nordstrom person. He said that he was a salesman who could work anywhere and sell anything, and that he would follow her career wherever it took her. This was our first experience with an enlightened male.

Betsy moved to Orange County to blaze the trail for Nordstrom outside the Pacific Northwest. Back then, to the average shopper in California, Nordstrom was an unknown. People in the retail industry were starting to get to know us, but few customers had heard of us outside the Northwest. Some people confused us with Norge, the refrigerator manufacturer. In anticipation of the opening, we ran some ads in the local newspapers.

We officially opened the store on May 1, 1978. At 127,000 square feet, it was bigger than the typical Nordstrom store at that time. Boy, I was so nervous that I thought I was going to throw up. I felt the pre-game tension. We had plenty of competition: Sears, May Company, Joseph Magnin, and Bullock's, with Saks Fifth Avenue opening in early 1979.

As we were getting ready to open the doors for the first time, there was virtually nobody in the mall. My cousins and I went back into the store and had some employees go out into the mall corridor and pretend to be shoppers. When our lone celebrity, the mayor of Costa Mesa, cut the ribbon, the only people in the audience who were applauding were Nordstrom employees. We have since learned how to open stores with guns blazing, but on that day, they were as blazing as we knew how to do it then. (We learned as the years went by that the more fuel we dumped on the fire, the more it blazed.)

I'm going to oversimplify opening day, but this is the heart of it: A few people started straggling in that morning. Later on in the day, more and more people started coming in. Why did the traffic in our store increase? My theory is that it was as simple as this: The first customers came in and were impressed. They went home and called their friends and told them to get down to South Coast Plaza to check out the new kid on the block. By the middle of that first day, our store was filled with smiling people.

All of us have stood on sales floors for a long time, so we know the difference between a store that's cooking and a store that is not cooking. We were cooking. We saw that South Coast Plaza was going to work right from the first day. After about three hours, you could go around from register to register and add it up.

Orange County is full of serious shoppers, and to a retailer, it's Valhalla; it's the Promised Land. The people of Southern California are great consumers, and I say that with all the respect in the world. Our success at South Coast Plaza showed us that we could go just about anyplace we wanted to. It gave us lots of confidence.

That year, our company-wide sales performance was outstanding. Our rate of growth really took off, and our price–earnings ratio was very good.

We started to attract notice and gain credibility. One of the most important national articles about us was in *Forbes* in 1978, titled "Bloomies in the Boonies." All of a sudden, some of the analysts started to get it, and Wall Street rewarded us for being different. Initially, the analysts didn't like us because we were too different. Because we were decentralized and emphasized customer service, they figured that we had a high-expense model. But when they began to realize that our model worked, we became a major player, and the rest, as they say, is history.

Betsy Sanders expertly pulled off our invasion of Southern California, which she ran all by herself. Betsy is a feisty soul, extremely competitive, and she wanted desperately to be top dog. At the time, to have someone

With Henry Segerstrom, who developed and owns South Coast Plaza, in 2006

of her gender in such a powerful position was so unusual that she became a media darling. Magazines, newspapers, and television news programs clamored to interview her.

Betsy eventually left our company, went on to become a consultant on customer service, and served as a director on many major corporate boards, including Wal-Mart, WellPoint, Carl's Jr., and Washington Mutual. Betsy is the best hire I ever made — and arguably the best hire that anybody has ever made.

Today, South Coast Plaza, which is a much bigger store in a much expanded mall, continues to be our top performer. I give Henry Segerstrom a tremendous amount of credit for staying the course and making sure that his family stayed with the shopping center. Few families own shopping centers anymore; insurance companies and real estate investment trusts own them. Not only did the Segerstrom family keep their center, but it's still the best. They spend a lot of money keeping South Coast Plaza special, but they get more rent than anybody else because they do more business than anybody else.

Bob joined Best's Apparel in 1947 and eventually became manager of Best's downtown Portland store. He started working for Nordstrom with the acquisition of Best's and stayed with the company until his retirement in 1978. He was one of the very few Best's employees who made a significant mark at Nordstrom.

Best's belonged to the New York buying office Specialty Stores Associated, along with other specialty-apparel retailers around the country. When Nordstrom bought Best's, Lloyd, who had never bought apparel, took me with him to New York to a buyers' meeting at Specialty Stores Associated. All the buyers from the other stores were helpful and pleasant, but their attitude toward Lloyd was patronizing, as if they were saying, "We're going to teach you how to do the business."

Lloyd was very polite all the way through, and after the last meeting he thanked everybody. When we left, he turned to me and said, "Bob, we're going to show them how to run a store." We did.

Nicholas Ungar was a high-end apparel store in downtown Portland, catering to the carriage trade. Every night, the store manager would gather up the cash and take it to the bank for new money so Ungar customers wouldn't have to touch dirty money. They even polished all the coins. When Nordstrom acquired Nicholas Ungar, we stopped doing that, which made for some unhappy customers, who couldn't understand why Nordstrom didn't become more like Ungar.

Lloyd said to me, "Let's tell everybody in Portland what we're doing," so we worked with a public relations outfit on a letter that would explain to the public what our business was all about. Lloyd read the letter and said to me, "This is good." Then he tore it up into little pieces and tossed them into the wastebasket. "Now," he said, "get out on the sales floor and tell them how we do it at Nordstrom."

BETSY SANDERS

Betsy joined the company in September 1971, rose through our organization, and opened up Southern California for us, eventually becoming general manager of that region. I consider Betsy the best hire I ever made.

In the 1970s, the Nordstroms started to recognize the important qualities of women in the organization — gravitas, commitment, connection with the customer. Many companies choose women for all the wrong reasons; the Nordstroms chose people who didn't see this as just a job; it was all about passion, commitment, and a willingness to break molds. Nordstrom, at its best, keeps re-creating the relationship with the customer. There's no script. God forbid! It's using best judgment at all times.

In January 1972, four months after I joined the company, I became the manager of a new department. I'll never forget a managers' meeting that I attended at the Washington Athletic Club where, for me, the Nordstrom Way was really set in concrete. At the time, we had recently gone public, we had had a good year in a terrible economy, and we were feeling pretty good about ourselves. At this meeting, we were looking at our goals for the next year.

The Nordstroms said, "We're afraid we're buying our own publicity instead of looking inward. There's only one goal that this company has to have in order for us to survive, much less thrive: We have to be the very best at customer service, by any standard. We know that you can't do it by yourselves, so we're going to help you in every way we can."

I was sitting there, a four-month employee, a brand-new manager, listening to every word they said, and I took it for gospel. Sometimes, at crucial times, it helps to be new.

When I left the company 20 years later, our number one goal was still the same: to be the very best at customer service.

CHAPTER 16

PRESS ON

All our success took a backseat in 1984, when my wife, Fran, died after a long and valiant fight with cancer. Losing Fran was the most catastrophic thing that ever happened to me. I can't think of anything worse.

Fran deserves tremendous credit, if not all the credit, for how great our three boys are. She was the best mom of all the moms. For the first 12 years that my sons were alive, she was the more dominant parent, the most significant influence in their developmental years. (When she got sick for the first time, and the boys were beginning to mature, I became more of an influence in their teenage years.) She drove the kids around in our wood-paneled station wagon, baked cookies, and made sure all the kids came to our house after school. Our kids weren't getting in trouble because either they were turning out for sports or they and all their friends were at our house. That was because of Fran. She cared so much about them and me, and I learned so much from her. Ed Pepple, the basketball coach at Mercer Island High School, called her the "Rock of Gibraltar" behind the scenes.

While I was working, Fran was giving back to the community. For 20 years, she did volunteer work at Children's Orthopedic Hospital (which is known today as Children's Hospital and Regional Medical Center), particularly in the recreational therapy department. She was a member of the hospital's board of trustees and served two years as chairman of the ways and means committee, which explored fund-raising methods for the hospital's guilds. She was active in Mercer Island's Little Dribblers basketball program when our boys were small, as well as Boys & Girls Clubs of King County (the first woman to be named to that board), the Junior League, and the boards of United Way and the Northwest Oncology Foundation.

She was the best mom of all the moms.

Fran in 1957

Looking back, I'm so regretful that I did not acknowledge Fran more and spend more quality time with her.

When I lost Fran, I went through clinical depression. I just couldn't pull myself out of it, and I wasn't very productive at work. My cousin Jim came into my office one day and said, "You're no good to anybody in the funk you're in." He talked me into taking up golf because, he said, it's so hard that you have to think about it. He was right, and it helped a lot.

We had this nice home on Mercer Island, but the boys were all gone by this time. I was just rattling around the house, which was a dark and lonely place to come home to at night.

Fortunately, I'm blessed with a lot of friends. At first, everybody is wonderful to you and they bring over casseroles and such, but that doesn't last forever, and pretty soon you're alone. I learned that I'm one of these guys who needs a wife; I'm horrible by myself. The only thing I could cook was bacon and eggs, which I'd have for dinner all the time. I couldn't get the bacon to come out with the eggs, so I'd eat out of the pan.

The people who most helped me get through this period, who saved my life, were my best friends Jack and Nancy Rodgers. It is hard for me to overemphasize what they meant to me. They were even there for me when I didn't want to see anybody, including them. Virtually every night, they'd invite me for dinner, and when I'd say, "I think I'll stay home," they'd say, "No, you're not. You're going to come over here. We're going to have burgers for dinner."

I'd go to their home even when I didn't want to because I always felt better when I did. I knew that I had to start feeling better because I wasn't going to be able to function if I didn't.

Jack and Nancy and I talked about a lot of things. They weren't afraid to talk about Fran, and I wasn't afraid to talk to them about her. It was sad, but it was constructive sad.

Pat and Helen Stusser, who also lived on Mercer Island, were another couple who provided me with no-questions-asked, loving support during this time. They remained wonderful friends for many years, and it was a sad time when Pat passed away.

I was also incredibly fortunate to have received counseling from my friend The Reverend Dr. Dale Turner, who at that time was the leader of the University Congregational United Church of Christ in Seattle, where he served for 24 years. Dale became a part of our family. He presided over Fran's funeral and counseled me afterward. I could never repay him for what he did for me. He married Blake and Molly, Erik and Julie, and Jeannie and me. He also baptized my grandkids.

I had met Dale when we were both on the board of Seattle Goodwill. (I eventually served a term as president.) At the time, our local Goodwill, which is arguably the best in the country, was required to pay a significant fee to be associated with the national Goodwill organization. We business types on the board all voted to quit the national Goodwill because we believed that our first priority was to serve the people of Seattle. Dale, who didn't want to disagree with anybody, said that rather than quit the national organization, we should help other Goodwills do better. We resigned for about a year and then we went right back with the national Goodwill. It turned out that Dale was right; we shouldn't have resigned. We were able to help the national because of our presence.

Dale, who originally intended to be a high school football coach, attended West Virginia Wesleyan (which is also the alma mater of my wife, Jeannie), where he was a star athlete, with the nickname Zeke, and later graduated from Yale Divinity School. He spent 10 years in Lawrence, Kansas, home of the University of Kansas, where he met Jack Rodgers, who later became my best friend. At the time, Jack was a quarterback on the UK football team and a guard on the basketball team, where he played with Dean Smith, who went on to become the legendary basketball coach of the University of North Carolina Tar Heels. Jack and Dale reconnected when they both found themselves in Seattle.

Until the day he died, in June 2006, at age 88, Dale Turner was one of the most important figures in my life; to me, he was like a saint on earth. For 22 years, he wrote the religion column in the *Seattle Times*. In one of his writings, entitled "Press On," he quoted Calvin Coolidge:

Nothing in the world can take the place of persistence. Talent will not. Nothing is more common than unsuccessful men with talent. Genius will not. Unrewarded genius is almost a proverb. Education alone will not. The world is full of educated derelicts. Persistence and determination alone are omnipotent.

These are words that I would like to live by. I don't all the time, but I wish I did.

A friend once said to me, "I don't get it. I've known you all my life and I've known your two wives. How could somebody like you get two like that?"

MY JEANNIE

In the early 1980s, while Fran was still alive, I had committed to be the head of the King County United Way campaign. For the first year, I served an apprenticeship, running the retail division's fund-raising. Jeannie O'Roark was my staff person, and it quickly became obvious that she was hardworking and effervescent, with a great personality. I just thought she was a terrific gal. She and Fran became friends, and that has given me a lot of comfort over the years.

A year and a half after Fran died, I asked Jeannie out, and I came to deeply love this most thoughtful of persons. We married in 1988, four years after Fran passed away. Jeannie is admired and cherished by all those whose lives she has touched, especially by me because of what she has meant in my life.

Besides her work with United Way, Jeannie has served on the board and has been the president of the YWCA of Seattle, King County, and Snohomish County, and has been deeply involved in raising money for the construction of the Y's new downtown building, Opportunity Place, which serves the needs of women of all ages, races, and faiths, and their families. Through Opportunity Place, the YWCA provides services to help end homelessness, create jobs, care for children and youths, and prevent violence. It's a haven for people who need safety and help in their lives. When Jeannie was president, they raised $40 million in funding, which was the largest "ask" in the history of Seattle philanthropic giving for a social services agency.

With Jeannie in 2005

Jeannie is admired and cherished by all those whose lives she has touched, especially by me because of what she has meant in my life.

She has served on the board of the Market Foundation, which helps to support the Pike Place Market's services for low-income people, including its clinic, senior center, food bank, and child care and preschool. She was on the board of IslandWood, a unique 255-acre educational facility on Bainbridge Island that offers programs and learning experiences to inspire people of all ages to be involved in environmental and community stewardship.

Jeannie's passion is saving unwanted animals. Working with the Humane Society and other organizations such as Purrfect Pals, we have had over 500 kittens go through the back bedroom of our condo over the years. She takes care of the mother and the litter until the kittens are old enough to be adopted. She's like an angel to these animals. We have always had dogs and cats in our condo, and at our cabin, Jeannie has rescued goats, burros, and a miniature horse.

Jeannie has often remarked that although she skipped having children, she is so fortunate to have five grandchildren. I believe they are so lucky to have her as well. She's the best grandma in the world.

On the day that Jeannie and I married (with Dale Turner officiating), I became whole again. I consider myself the luckiest guy I know. I have been really blessed. She has taught me so much about humanity, truly caring about others, and compassion for all living things, and has reconfirmed for me how wonderful life is.

A friend once said to me, "I don't get it. I've known you all my life and I've known your two wives. How could somebody like you get two like that?"

I said, "The good Lord knew I needed help and he sent me two. That's all I can attribute it to."

My Jeannie, in 1990

A scene from a typical store opening

Our philosophy has always been to go in with **guns blazing**, hit the ground running.

CHAPTER 17

BECOMING A
NATIONAL COMPANY

As the 1970s drew to a close, we were no longer a big secret to the rest of the country. By 1980, we were the third-largest specialty retailer in the nation, behind Saks Fifth Avenue and Lord & Taylor. We had 31 stores in California, Washington, Oregon, and Alaska, with annual sales per square foot of $187, about twice the industry average. We continued to concentrate a good portion of our expansion in California, and by the early 1980s, California accounted for about 25 percent of our sales. In 1985, to show our commitment to California, we held our annual shareholders meeting in Palo Alto — the first time we had ever done that outside Seattle.

Around that time, Sam Walton paid me one of the greatest compliments I've ever received when he asked me to be on the board of Wal-Mart, which was still mostly a regional player in the South. I respectfully declined. My rejoinder to Mr. Sam was "One day, you and I are going to be competitors."

"Oh, no," he said. "We're just a little company down in the South selling low-price goods. You're a big company on the West Coast selling better-price merchandise."

I said, "We're not going to stay just on the West Coast, and I know you're not staying in the South." Of course, they were on their way to becoming the largest retailer in the world.

Our first 60 full-line stores were designed by Barden "Bud" Erickson, my old Beta fraternity brother and our vice president for store design. Bud was a founder of the Seattle-based architectural firm The Callison Partnership. Bud did his job better than any other executive in any other capacity in the history of our company.

We truly became a national company on March 4, 1988, when we opened our first East Coast store, a 211,000-square-foot showplace at Tysons Corner Center in McLean, Virginia, a suburb of Washington, D.C. The following year, we opened a 241,000-square-foot store at the Fashion Centre at Pentagon City, in Arlington, Virginia.

To us, the Washington, D.C., area was an East Coast version of Orange County; it was the place to be. What makes that region so good? Number one: Washington, D.C., has distinct seasons, which helps the retail business. Number two: There are lots of opportunities for dressing up. With the Kennedy Center and other facilities, Washington has a vast array of cultural and civic events; and because it's a town full of politicians, lobbyists, and special-interest groups, there is a banquet or party virtually every night of the year.

Nevertheless, going to the East Coast wasn't easy because of the cultural differences and shopping habits of customers. Shoppers there are more creatures of habit than those in California, who want to see the newest thing. But our level of customer service set us apart.

For example, the night of a big society ball, a customer called our Pentagon City store and said that he couldn't tie the bow tie for his tuxedo. One of our people said, "C'mon down and I'll tie it for you." The customer drove to the parking lot, stuck his head out of his car window, and got his tie tied. We received lots of great media coverage from that.

Our first East Coast store, at Tysons Corner Center
in Virginia, opened in 1988.

Store managers carry our culture in their heart and soul.

In 1990, we finally made it into the New York area, with a store in the Garden State Plaza in Paramus, New Jersey. To introduce ourselves, we ran two full-page ads in *The New York Times*: "If the shoe fits, you've already discovered Nordstrom." And "New York has it all. Almost." We got great results. People from New York like shopping in New Jersey, where there is no sales tax on apparel. Those first few years, a significant percentage of our business came from New Yorkers.

The success of a new store in a new market is ultimately the responsibility of the store manager. The managers carry our culture in their heart and soul. I still say that Betsy Sanders set the template. It's up to us in management to (1) select the best people, and (2) hold their feet to the fire and make sure that our point of difference is being translated in their town.

I firmly believe that the culture happens one day at a time and one sale at a time. That's why our reputation is so fragile.

We were fortunate that John Whitacre was our guy when we opened up Tysons because he understood our culture. We made an unbelievable splash in Washington, D.C., comparable to what Betsy did in Southern California. D.C. was probably harder because people come there from everywhere, and it is more of a cultural melting pot. John built the core, which allowed us to add several more stores in that area.

It's important to note that all our managers come from existing stores. Over the years, we've learned that great Nordstrom store managers and regional managers come in all shapes and sizes and colors and genders. We try to pick people who have proved that they can honor the qualities that built our business and culture. They have to be both strong and humble — strong because they have to delegate responsibility, and humble because they are newcomers to the area, and need to get new people on their side. Managers must create a level of expectation and excitement, beginning with the first people they hire.

Some good department managers don't become good store managers. They can still be a Nordy, with an understanding of what we're trying to do, but they may not have the ability or confidence to delegate responsibility and to empower their people. A good store manager must be able to trust others because it's impossible to micromanage one of our stores; there are too many moving parts.

STORE OPENINGS

Our store openings are always exciting. I get a thrill seeing customers, with a look of rapture on their faces, lining up to rush into the store. If only we could sustain that feeling every day.

These new-store openings are very costly, with a huge initial expense. Our philosophy has always been to go in with guns blazing, hit the ground running, make it a community event. We always want to sell from a full cart — that means lots of inventory — no matter what, but especially when we open a store. But with a new store, even though we don't know what the sales level is going to be, we set a sales goal and we buy the inventory to achieve that goal. Since our goal is generally higher than what we achieve, we often end up with too much inventory. Fortunately, our company is now large enough that we can pretty quickly balance out that excess inventory and redistribute it to our other stores. We don't like to send stuff back to the vendor when we don't have to, and we feel that if we created the over-inventory situation, then we should live with it. Many other retailers don't do that.

We like to start off on the right foot, to give back something to the community before we open our doors. We will have a pre-opening fund-raising event for local charities, which will create a crowd. (The charities, of course, get 100 percent of the proceeds.) Over the years, we have helped to raise many millions of dollars for good causes all over the country.

By the way, when an existing store has bogged down and is having morale problems or flat sales, I'll say, "To re-energize the employees, let's pretend we are opening for the first time next month and do the same things we do when we are opening a store: more seminars, more product-knowledge meetings, more tips on how to sell." When employees see that managers are doing everything they can to drive the business, that creates good morale.

Our biggest store opening up to that time — in terms of the actual size — occurred in October 1988. We built an unusual store that begins on the fourth floor of a vertical mall and goes up through the seventh floor, covering 350,000 square feet at the San Francisco Centre on Lower Market Street. One of the features of the Centre is its circular escalator, and for many years, we were the only retailer in the country that had one.

That store was a gamble, not only the way it was set up, but also its location, a formerly seedy stretch of downtown that at the time was not an area where our customers wanted to shop. We were unable to get a site around Union Square, and that's where our competition was. On the positive side, the city was involved in a tremendous urban-renewal project that included all of the city's services on the same side of Market (a very wide street that accommodates a lot of traffic) where our store is located.

Most important, San Francisco is, after all, San Francisco — a great city with a great downtown. The cable car turnaround was right in front of our store, which made it an ideal tourist-oriented location. We were confident that we could do something unusual in a place that attracted customers. We were right. San Francisco Centre continues to be one of our best-performing stores.

*For more than 50 years, Hazel Martin embodied the
Nordstrom spirit for us in Portland, Oregon.*

We are often asked how we find people
who want to give our level of customer
service. Most of the time, they find us.

CHAPTER 18

HIRING, KEEPING, AND PROMOTING THE RIGHT PEOPLE

We are blessed in that we have many more job applicants than we have openings, which is a great indicator that we treat people well and have a successful company. We are often asked how we find people who want to give our level of customer service. Most of the time, they find us. Some people might think our way of doing things is too gung ho for them. Okay, then don't work here. This is not a job for clock-watchers.

For the most part, I'm a disbeliever in job interviews, which I think can be seriously misleading. Perhaps people more sensitive than I can divine right from wrong from an interview, but nobody is able to look somebody in the eye and predict how successful that person will be in our business. You can't just take what this person says at face value. In an interview, people say what they think you want to hear. The guy may have shined his shoes only once in a year, and it's the day he comes in and talks to you.

I tell our folks that when they are hiring within our company for a new job, or promoting someone from one department to another, the single best thing they can do — before they ever say a word to a job candidate — is to run a "background check." Call up the manager that person is working for and get his or her opinion. You'll find out everything, including the warts. Nothing wrong with that; we all have warts.

A good candidate has persistence and tenacity. If a young person applies for a job here but doesn't get hired, does she refuse to take no for an answer? Does she come back again and again? Does she show you that she really wants the job? If the answer to all three of those questions is yes, then that's the person I want on my team.

Our employees — now 50,000 strong — must have an understanding and appreciation of our culture. Building a genuine, good culture is necessary for long-lasting success.

We have been fortunate to attract outstanding people who are responsive to our entrepreneurial culture. The caliber of the people we attract today is so much higher, as is their level of education. Even so, when a student from Southern California wrote me a letter asking what level of education she needed to succeed in our company, I told her, "You don't have to have much formal education to be successful. There are no barriers."

Identifying the up-and-comers is probably the biggest job we have. Once we've identified them, we watch them very closely and track their results. They know we're watching, and they either rise to those expectations or they don't.

Because of our reputation for service, many people think we're magic at training. But three days is the most we spend on training. It's very perfunctory. We are strong believers in on-the-job training, and we carefully monitor the performance of new hires to make sure they are doing the job the Nordstrom way.

After going through training and orientation, people are full of good intentions, but they're nervous. Let's say a bright young woman gets sent to the sportswear department to sell. She gets off the escalator and walks over to the department. Ideally, this is what she sees:

- A busy department
- Salespeople engaging the customers in a personal conversation
- Salespeople coming out from behind the wrap desk to hand the customers their packages
- Salespeople carrying packages out to the car for a customer

These new hires will see firsthand the level of performance they will have to reach to make it at Nordstrom. They are being inspired by the highest common denominator.

In our culture, people raise themselves up to another level.

Once salespeople are hired, we measure them, right off the reel, by their production. We are a **results-oriented** company, and sales are what keep us in business.

Conversely, let's say that same young person gets a job at a rival department store. She starts work with the same good intentions — to be successful, to make some money, to do the right thing. On her first day of work, she gets off the escalator and what does she see? Probably not many salespeople and not many customers. A couple of salespeople are standing behind the wrap desk, chewing gum, talking to each other, or talking to a friend on the phone. She goes into the back room and hears people bitching about the last customer they had, and subconsciously she thinks, "Oh, that's how things work around here." The lowest common denominator.

In our culture, people raise themselves up to another level. We don't want somebody just punching a clock.

When we hire those eager beavers, it would be a crime if we didn't feed them while they're hungry. Over the years, we've done more and more mentoring for people at the entry level. Newcomers get a quick understanding of what we're trying to do, but some of them don't buy into it. If you lay it out for them, via a mentor, the people who have it within themselves are more apt to buy into our deal. We want our good people, our proven performers, to be nice and helpful to new people. Unfortunately, some of the real star salespeople don't want to mentor. They get protective of their turf and don't want to cut anybody in on it. Rather than "waste" their time helping someone else, they'd rather spend all their time on their own production. Fortunately, most top salespeople are more apt to be team players.

Once salespeople are hired, we measure them, right off the reel, by their production. We are a results-oriented company, and sales are what keep us in business.

Retail is a high-energy business, and you have to have the desire from deep within you. It's a sweaty business and it requires a lot of hours. You can be smart and a hard worker, but you don't have to be a genius. You don't have to have professional training, as you would for accounting or engineering. It's on-the-job training.

In the first six months, we turn over a lot of new hires. But if you get what we're doing, and you can last a year or two, we are the best retailer for retaining people.

We have a high level of expectation in this company. We keep on raising the bar. The winners jump over the bar; the losers knock the bar off.

I want our frontline people to have pride in themselves. A lot of that has to do with their having pride in us. They have to respect where they work and who they work for before they can have respect for themselves. And we have to have respect for them. It's a neat circle, really.

Increases are the lifeblood of our business; we must always have increases in our comparable figures from year to year. That's unrelenting. Every day, we want every person with any kind of responsibility in this company to know the numbers he or she has to go against and how to make the numbers that single day. In order to make your numbers, there should be a sense of urgency each and every day.

Dale Cameron, who ran our cosmetics division for many years until she retired in 2006, was arguably our best merchant. I'd see her every morning, and she would tell me how yesterday was and what was going on today. Dale was terrific at planning and focusing and making sure there was something going on in every department for every day. It can be wearing, but for Dale, it was part of her DNA.

When I was a department manager, we had to carry in our breast pocket a card that had the volume of every day of the month for the previous year. For example, you have your card for January all filled out, and then each day you write in what you did on the corresponding day this year.

Retail is a business
of optimism.

Why do you do that? Because you're keeping score. You've got to sell more than you did the year before. I wish we did a little more of that these days. In the old days, all the managers in our company had that scorecard in their pocket.

Retail is a business of optimism. If you are optimistic, you plan for sales to be at a certain target level, so you buy inventory to justify those sales. Until our customers tell us otherwise, we have to think that we are forever gaining. We plan for gains and we expect to gain.

You have to be goal oriented to be in this business. There was no better example of that in our organization than Dave Butler, who was a great shoe salesman in Tacoma. He and his wife were quite a pair. Before the start of every year, they would map out in great detail what it was going to take for him to achieve his goals. She'd often call him at 11 o'clock in the morning and ask, "What do you have up so far?" If he was behind the goal, she'd say, "Then you must get on it!" This is not an exaggeration.

One day, I was at the Tacoma store when Dave, who never missed a day, was sick. He called his wife and told her he'd better go home. She said, "No, you stay there and make the day. I'll take care of you tonight."

That's goal-setting to the nth degree. No wonder Dave was the best shoe salesman in our company.

John Pedrini, the 2006 John W. Nordstrom Award winner,
is shown with Pete, Blake, Erik, and their cousin Jamie.

We are at our best when we **recognize** good performance.

CHAPTER 19

RECOGNITION AND PRAISE

I believe in the old bromide "Congratulate people in groups. Criticize people one by one." No sense trotting somebody up in front of his peers and calling him a dope.

Our training, which is on-the-job training, is only as good as the people entrusted with that responsibility — not just our good HR department (which is composed of people we really lean on), but also our department managers, assistant managers, store managers, and so on, who do the lion's share of the real training. They have discovered that personal, one-on-one mentoring is the best tool to impart our culture.

We are at our best when we recognize good performance. Our best salespeople achieve the status of Pacesetter, which means they rank among the top 10 percent of our salespeople in each division. Each department sets a Pacesetter goal, and salespeople who achieve this goal receive a house 33 percent discount for the year.

Pacesetters who surpass $1 million in annual sales volume become members of the Million Dollar Club, which represents a very diverse group. The beauty of our company these days is that a large percentage of these super performers grew up outside the United States. It's neat to sit in a room with them and to hear them talking in different accents and inflections. They are so thrilled to be in America and to take advantage of the opportunity to work hard and succeed. They are always giving that something extra, and that special effort pays off for them. This is their chance to make it in America, just as my grandpa did more than a century ago.

These people possess the qualities that I think are essential to this business: alertness, tenacity, and consistency. They are prepared every day to do what needs to be done.

Recognition, particularly in front of peers, is the best incentive, outside of a raise. That recognition, which must be sincere and honest, is usually the job of individual department managers. During department meetings, the manager will single out one or two people in front of their peers, and will recount how these particular employees gave great service to a customer or a co-worker. The manager might even put a rose in the employee's lapel for the day. We tell people we reward that they are the kind of person we want others to emulate, that we value and cherish their input, and that we wouldn't be as successful without them. It's strong stuff.

We keep setting the bar higher for the people who want to be the very best, the people who hear about an award or an honor list or a contest and say, "I want to win that!"

When individuals and departments are on target for reaching their sales goals, they are praised over the store intercom during the morning announcements before the store opens. We reward outstanding sales-per-hour and sales-per-month performance with cash prizes or trips, awards, and public praise.

Why are we constantly finding ways to praise and recognize our people? Because selling is tough. Sometimes you're dealing with angry and complaining customers who are yelling at you. Believe me, I know from experience. We have so many good folks who have made a career of this, and it's up to us to provide them some uplift as they work day after day, week after week, year after year.

At our monthly recognition meetings, employees are honored for things such as departmental sales increases and promotional ideas that drive sales increases. These meetings are probably the biggest morale boosters in our company because they also double as pep rallies.

We also recognize customer service, which is the one thing that differentiates us from every other retailer out there. We've had a lot of people who were in the middle of the pack in terms of sales numbers, but who gave exceptional service and had a loyal clientele. The contributions of people who give exceptional customer service are just as valuable as the contributions of people who sell the most merchandise in the department. We need everybody — not just Pacesetters — performing well. So every month, store managers select their Customer Service All-Stars, who are evaluated on outstanding, consistent customer service and the level of support and teamwork they give their co-workers. If you're not a team player, you won't have a long career at Nordstrom.

Many times at the recognition meetings, these All-Stars are surprised by the presence of their parents or spouse and children. It's a very emotional experience. The people who attend these meetings get so charged up, they take that energy back to their departments, and it spreads throughout the company.

HONESTY AND INTEGRITY

Honesty and integrity are essential to the success of our culture, so you can't cut corners to inflate your sales numbers. People who try to "jimmy" the system eventually get caught and are terminated because that kind of behavior can't be tolerated. For example, many years ago we had a fellow who ran a very small leased shoe department for us. He was as impressive a guy as you'd ever meet, and he worked his tail off. All of a sudden he was having incredible sales increases, and we wondered how he was doing it. We eventually learned that, after working all day in the department he managed, he would drive to the main store in Seattle and pull inventory from the stockroom — without doing the paperwork for transferring the inventory. He took those shoes and sold them in the department he managed in his store. Once we discovered what he was doing, we had to fire him. It was sad. His moral compass was off a little bit.

In the pursuit of a sale, when you're waiting on a customer, you might be tempted to say, "Gee, that dress looks great on you," but it might really look awful. Remember, customers appreciate honesty. They'd rather hear you say something like "That dress doesn't go with your coloring. Why not try this item instead?"

It's not being dishonest to sell people all that they want to buy. Use your honesty and hard work to present the merchandise in the best possible light.

Dishonesty also means pretending to know more than you actually do. When you are a salesperson, there is a real temptation to embellish your

If you're not a team player, you won't have a long career at Nordstrom.

knowledge and pretend to be an expert. I know, because I was tempted by that a few times myself. If you say, "I don't know the answer, but I'll find out for you and I'll be right back," customers will appreciate and respect you.

Back in the 1950s, we had a real character on our staff at our Rhodes leased shoe department. One day, a woman came into the store and asked to see "the doctor."

I said, "We don't have any doctors around here."

She said, "Yes you do. That fellow right over there," pointing to a salesman named Jack.

I went over to Jack and said, "You're not telling these ladies you're a doctor, are you?"

He said, "I'm telling them I'm a doctor of fitting shoes."

We put an end to that.

One day, he told me he wasn't feeling well and had to go home early. I had a hunch about this guy. I went into the stockroom of Rhodes, which had a window facing First Avenue, and when I looked out the window, I saw him crossing the street to a tavern.

Every salesman was responsible for keeping his stock clean and neat, and this fellow's stock was not in very good shape. One time while he was gone, I asked the stockboy to tighten his stock. The stockboy pulled a box of shoes out of the shelf and I heard a "clank." In the box was a bottle of booze and a glass. Obviously, we had to part ways.

JOHN W. NORDSTROM AWARD

Every year since 1961, our family has honored a Nordstrom manager (who is not an officer at that time) who best exemplifies the characteristics of our founder with the John W. Nordstrom Award, the highest honor in our company. The winners demonstrate hard work, persistence, servant leadership, loyalty, honesty, strong ethics, competitive spirit, and perhaps most important, an unwavering commitment to put the customer first. It is not for one week, one month, or one year, but rather for every single day that person comes to work. In addition, this person must have gone through the inevitable ups and downs of our business, while consistently delivering great results over time. With our company having grown to approximately 50,000 employees, this is quite a special award.

The winner is chosen by our family. Until a few years ago, John, Jim, Jack, and I went into a room, closed the door, and evaluated candidates. We solicited some input from outside, but we were still close enough to the business and it was small enough that we knew most of the people personally.

Today, John W. Nordstrom's great-grandsons Blake, Pete, Erik, and Jamie actively solicit nominations from our regional heads, who in turn get them from the store managers. There is less reliance on gut feeling and more reliance on facts and numbers. You have to have good numbers, but you also have to do your business with a smile and do whatever you're asked to do in a cooperative way. We've passed on people who have had good results but perhaps complained too much or were not great team players. In the end, the determining factor is a selfless dedication to what our company is all about.

The identity of the winner is a closely held secret, to maintain the surprise element of the selection, which is announced at a regularly scheduled regional recognition meeting. While the regional manager is conducting the meeting, all of a sudden here come these four tall funny-looking Swedes — Blake, Pete, Erik, and Jamie — and everybody knows that something's up. The winner is announced, and here come his or her spouse and children, whom we secretly notified beforehand. It becomes a joyous occasion for everybody, and there's not a dry eye in the house. It's just as much fun for us as it is for the winners and their peers.

Every year, previous John W. Nordstrom winners meet for a big bash at a fancy restaurant. We honor them and their accomplishments, and the whole group honors the newest recipient. With the old-timers, we reminisce about the old days. It's our way of thanking them, for they are the ones who have enabled us to get this far.

I think of past winners such as Gale Wergeland, Tex Hartley, Bob Goodson, Weldy Johnson, Winnie Clay, Harold Wolslegel, Sue Tabor, Jammie Baugh, and Bill Noble, who did a variety of jobs throughout the company. This is just a small sampling of the irreplaceable people who have won this award. They carried the spear; they were us.

JOHN W. NORDSTROM AWARD WINNERS

Fall 1961	Fran Buchanan
Spring 1962	C. H. Griffith
Fall 1962	Rauley Fox
Spring 1963	Tom Gardiner
Fall 1963	Houston Hartley
Spring 1964	Allan Goesling
Fall 1964	Harold Wolslegel
Spring 1965	Weldon Johnson
Fall 1965	Wesley Harris
Spring 1966	Gussie Geller
Fall 1966	Adolph Frank
Spring 1967	Norm Sadis
Fall 1967	Ernie Carino
1968	Gale Wergeland
1969	Winnie Clay
1970	Helen Schreiber
1971	Bill Noble
1972	Bob Weil
1973	Lillian Clark
1974	Bob Nunn
1975	LaVerne Palmer
1976	Bob Goodson
1977	Wayne Badovinus
1978	Jack McDonald
1979	Anne Gilbert

1980	Akiko Akagi
1981	Tom Bosch
1982	Darrel Hume
1983	Blanqui Roeber
1984	Bob Sims
1985	John Whitacre
1986	Sue Tabor
1987	Jill (Dooley) Early
1988	Brian Tatsumura
1989	Jammie Baugh
1990	Pat Kennedy
1991	Debbie Geddes
1992	Steve Schreiber
1993	Joleen Davis
1994	Vicki McWilliams
1995	Joel Stinson
1996	Tim Gary
1997	Kathy Moser
1998	Trent Kamman
1999	Stephanie Friel
2000	Jackie Schell
2001	Pat Smith
2002	Brent Harris
2003	Leslie Martin
2004	Annette Tauber
2005	Pat McGowan
2006	John Pedrini

*There were many employee rallies in support of
Nordstrom during the union showdown in 1990.*

They attacked us on our greatest strength

and our most fragile commodity —

our reputation.

CHAPTER 20

THE UNION STORY

Seattle had long been a big union town. Dave Beck, who was president of the Brotherhood of Teamsters in the 1950s, lived here.

Our company had "interesting" relations with the unions representing our workers in the Seattle area. Back in the 1930s, in the dark days of the Depression, Nordstrom was instrumental in getting the local shoe union started, and we encouraged our people in those efforts.

When I was a young man, I asked my dad why we were unionized, and he said that we should be, because shoe-selling was humbling and, at the time, not a very rewarding profession. Consequently, it was essential to raise the bar for the whole industry and improve the pay scale for these people. If the union did it, then all the stores would have to do it, and there would be an even playing field. Then, all things being equal, we would do better because we would sell more.

But as the years went by, my dad changed his mind about unions because they stopped being a partner in building our business and became an irritant, another hurdle to jump over in order to be successful. They tended to want things reduced to the lowest common denominator, which was counter to our goal of having our people make as much money as they could. When the union asked for an increase in the percentage of commission, we countered by saying that we would raise the employees' guarantee. Our reasoning was that every year, because of inflation, the price of the merchandise goes up, so salespeople can make more money on the same percentage of commission. That was a basic disagreement that we had with the union.

My uncle Elmer was the primary person when it came to union negotiations. He was good at it, although he had a bit of a temper. (Perhaps that temper helped him to be good at it.) His son John succeeded Elmer in this assignment, and I think John was better at it than his father.

When I was in college, we had our longest strike, which lasted 11 days, but we were able to keep the stores open. One night during that strike, Elmer was coming out of the store and ran into the business agent for the union, Johnny Gentile, who stormed up to Elmer and started yelling at him. Gentile was a short, fast-talking fellow who always had a cigar in his mouth. Without saying a word, Elmer, who towered over Gentile, grabbed the cigar out of his mouth, threw it on the ground, and said, "Don't you blow smoke in my face," and walked away.

During that same strike, my mother, my sister, and I kept the University store open. One day, Gentile was walking up and down the sidewalk in front of the store, carrying a big picket sign that proclaimed how unfair Nordstrom was. He really made my mother angry. All of a sudden, the skies opened up and we got one of those heavy Seattle rainstorms, with water coming down in buckets. Gentile ran for shelter under the covered outside foyer leading to the entrance of our store. That was enough for my mother, who told Gentile, "You get off this property right now!" He went back out in the rain, absolutely drenched.

A few years earlier, when I was 15, I was working in the downtown store during a Half-Yearly Sale and the store was packed. I was speeding up and down the aisles of the stockroom and all of a sudden, this hand reached out and grabbed me. I was face-to-face with this rough-looking character who said to me, "Who the hell are you?"

"I'm Bruce."

"Bruce who?"

"Bruce Nordstrom."

"We'll see about that." He stomped off. It was Johnny Gentile. Somebody must have told him I was Everett's son, and he came back and apologized. He knew I wasn't going to join his union.

THE 1990 SHOWDOWN

From those early days up through today, we continue to set the wage standard for Seattle retail workers. By the 1980s, we had become a national company, and the only stores in our chain that were unionized were the six in the Seattle-Tacoma market. In 1987, right before new contract talks were initiated with Local 1001 of the United Food and Commercial Workers Union (UFCW), many of our Seattle-area employees asked us to make union membership optional, which would have made us an "open shop" — as opposed to the existing situation, in which we were a closed shop and union membership was mandatory.

In our naïveté, we didn't realize that asking for an open shop was blasphemy to the union movement. The union fought back by alleging that we forced managers to make employees work extra hours for "non-selling" activities — such as writing thank-you notes, stocking inventory, attending meetings, and delivering merchandise to customers or to other stores — and not record those hours, which would have been a violation of Washington State wage-and-hour laws. We denied the charges.

The talks with the union dragged on. The contract expired in July 1989, and we had become, ipso facto, an open shop.

Rather than calling for a strike — which would not have been approved by our employees — the union waged a negative publicity campaign against us. They attacked us on our greatest strength and our most fragile commodity — our reputation. That's when we saw negative letters to the editor in the local newspapers and damning articles about us written by columnists who were inclined to support the union's point of view. Consequently, we didn't feel appreciated in our hometown, where for nine decades we had tried to be the best civic citizens we could be.

The union conflict was such a toxic thing, and sadly, some of our employees were a part of it. The most poisonous thing was the union hierarchy, who would have closed us down in a second if they thought they could get away with it. They were stirring things up and causing people to have negative thoughts about the culture of this company.

We had bomb threats. I personally got a phone call at three in the morning: "You sonofabitch, we're going to bomb you and blow up your house." Then they hung up.

In March 1990, the UFCW filed a class-action lawsuit against Nordstrom on behalf of 50,000 past and present employees in Washington, Oregon, California, Alaska, Utah, and Virginia, charging all sorts of unfair labor practices — which was untrue.

The negative public relations culminated with a biased, one-sided front-page article in *The Wall Street Journal* that was so full of hyperbole it was a joke. But this whole situation was no joke to us. It was deadly serious.

The union did damage to us, no question about it. On the other hand, it got our competitive juices flowing and became an incentive for us to perform at an even higher level.

Fortunately, we had a lot of employees on our side. Bud Erickson, our director of store planning and my old Beta fraternity brother, did a great job of rallying the troops.

Given all this negative publicity, my cousins and I traveled to many of our stores to apprise our people of what was going on. The essence of what we said to employees was this: "You guys make more money than your brethren in competitors' stores. So do our folks in Seattle. It's the same deal. Yet you don't have to pay dues and you're not in a union. We don't treat you any differently than we treat them." They were in a position to judge us daily as a business. We were asking them for their support, if in fact they thought we deserved it. And, of course, we got it.

A group of employees operating under the name Nordstrom Employees Opposed to Union Representation (NEOUR) were working on decertifying Local 1001. (The National Labor Relations Board could order a decertification election if more than 30 percent of employees petitioned for it, or if the company had evidence that more than 30 percent of members didn't want the union.)

NEOUR held rallies in Bellevue and Seattle and joined forces with employees who held rallies at our stores in San Francisco, Southern California, and Washington, D.C. NEOUR and other anti-union associates demonstrated in front of the stores, carrying signs reading "We Love Our Company" and wearing "Nobody Asked Us" buttons. In Seattle, more than 1,000 employees signed an ad that said, "We are proud to work for Nordstrom. We support our company, and the atmosphere of excellence it fosters." In Orange County, employees ran similar ads that were paid for entirely through voluntary contributions from more than 1,000 Nordstrom employees in that region.

This whole episode literally made me sick. One time, I was giving a talk down in Southern California and I was feeling awful. I went into a room to lie down, and I threw up blood and passed out. I don't know how long I lay there. I was by myself, and nobody knew what was happening to me. Turns out, I had a bleeding stomach. I felt like I was a hundred years old. The union deal almost killed me, literally.

We eventually got some very good public relations help from Dave Marriott, a local PR executive, who calmed us down and advised us on how to proceed and how to get our side of the story out to the public.

One day I got a call from a woman named Elizabeth who said she was from the *60 Minutes* news magazine on CBS. "We're going to do a story on you," she said.

"That's really nice of you, but we're going to pass," I responded.

She said, "You don't understand. We're going to do a story on you." She told me that they had been contacted by the UFCW and that they had heard we were unfair to our employees.

We went to our board of directors and discussed the situation. To a person, they said, "Do not be interviewed by these guys. Do not go on television because they'll make you look like a donkey. They have an agenda. You'll be quoted out of context."

We told the producers we wouldn't cooperate personally, but we gave them and their crew the run of the store. They could talk to anybody they wanted; they could go into any department they wanted; they could even go into the back room. If we had given them a specific list of people, it would have been obvious that they were company people.

That's when I came to respect *60 Minutes*, when I saw how much work goes into one 15-minute segment. They had cameramen, producers, directors, and writers all over the place.

I was dodging Elizabeth, the producer, who was tenacious. One day, I came out of the men's room and she was standing there waiting for me. "I'm going to give you one more chance," she said. "This is not looking good for you. You've got to give your side of the story. Morley Safer will be here tomorrow, and we'd like to do the interview with him the next day."

When I told her of the stories we had heard about being ambushed and being quoted out of context, she replied, "We're not Mike Wallace. We're Morley Safer," who she said was a fair guy. (We learned that each star reporter has his or her own team of producers and writers.)

I called an emergency meeting of the family to discuss whether we should agree to be interviewed on camera. We were all sweating bullets about this whole thing. Jim, Jack, and I voted to do it, but John voted against it in the strongest of terms. We had always agreed that if one of us felt so strongly about something, we wouldn't do it. When we were finally about to give in to him, he said, "If that's your decision, I support it."

We were offered the chance to meet with Morley Safer before the interview. We went to my new condo in downtown Seattle because we didn't want to be seen with him in public and he didn't want to be seen with us.

We were sitting there waiting for him, and boy, were we nervous. My wife, Jeannie, was there to see if she could help with things.

Morley Safer asked if we minded if he smoked, and we said, "No, of course not." Since we don't smoke, we didn't have any ashtrays, so Jeannie gave him a saucer. I think those were the only cigarettes ever smoked in our place.

Initially, he didn't come across as warm or easy to talk to. In fact, he preferred talking about himself, telling us about being a war correspondent in Vietnam and all the awards he'd won. We were sitting there, despairing, when suddenly our dog Stuffy, a funny little mutt, ran into the room and started scratching at Safer's leg, creating a cloud of hair and dandruff.

"Stuffy," I said, "get away from there!"

Safer picked up Stuffy, put him in his lap, began to pet him, and said, "I love dogs." Stuffy saved the day.

Safer said that although the union had made some serious allegations, we would be given the opportunity for rebuttal. He convinced us that he'd be fair, so we agreed to do the interview the following day. They filmed the four of us for about 90 minutes, and I ended up doing a lot of talking. I was passionate about all this, and I hope that passion came across.

Nevertheless, we assumed that the worst was going to happen. The show was originally scheduled to air the following week, but they ended up running it about six weeks later. We were dying the whole time.

The Sunday night that the show aired, I got a call from Jeannie's brother,

Jim O'Roark. He lives in Pittsburgh, so he was able to watch it three hours earlier than those of us on the West Coast. Jim said simply, "You got 'em!"

The segment about us started off with an interview with a former employee who had worked in the men's department at the Aurora Village store. Sadly, this young man had contracted AIDS, and he claimed that we let him go because of that, which we did not do. Because he was physically weak and couldn't stand on the sales floor, we said, "We won't cut your pay, but we will give you a different job, where you can sit and do paperwork." Instead, he quit. We brought that out in our rebuttal. The segment ended with that same young man, who was asked by Morley Safer if he would come back to Nordstrom if he were given the opportunity. He said he would do it in a minute.

That answer took all the wind out of the union's sails, and at that moment, we knew we had won. We felt that we had successfully conveyed our message, and there was a better feeling among employees and customers.

We made a last-second monetary settlement on the lawsuit, which was a small amount to get rid of the nuisance value. People warned us that if we took on the union on this issue, they would be after us every single year, but that has not been the case.

Today, we continue to have excellent relations with our people. My pitch is that management must treat employees well and with respect. Unions have a role in standing up for people who are being taken advantage of, but I'll go to my deathbed thinking that for this company and for many others in this country, unions have outlived their usefulness and have become a negative and not a positive in building industries and standards of living.

When the issues with the union were becoming voluminous and complicated, we needed a full-time person in Seattle to be a liaison between the company and our attorneys at Lane Powell. We selected Brooke White, who had been the head of HR at our South Coast Plaza store, the biggest store in our company, to fill the position we called "legal coordinator." She was just the person we needed to explain our jargon to the lawyers, and to provide them support on the lawsuit. Wayne Gittinger, our attorney and director, who is very hard to please and who has very high standards, told me, "You have a real star here."

Around the time that the lawsuit was resolved, we needed a new corporate public relations director, and we chose Brooke. None of us in the third generation believed in public relations, which we thought was a waste of time and money, but we knew that our company had reached a size at which it was important.

Brooke does a wonderful job at a task that doesn't have a big budget. We're not inclined to emotionally support public relations, but she gives us sound advice, counsel, and leadership, and has done a terrific job.

To give you an indication of our feeling about public relations, even before the *60 Minutes* episode, we were never comfortable dealing with the media and avoided coverage if at all possible. I remember when dear Norm Sadis was a young guy, and he was interviewed by *Footwear News*, the bible of our industry. A reporter asked him how the season was going. Norm got really enthusiastic and told the reporter, "We've had the best season on evening shoes. Even the ugly ones sold." When I saw that, I burned. I told Norm that we don't want to tell our competitors what's selling, and what's more, we don't want to show off. We try not to believe our own press clippings because too much praise is like a narcotic, and just as harmful.

Back in 1987, *Footwear News* named me their Man of the Year. I didn't want to take all the credit, so I didn't want to accept the award, and I didn't want to pose for a picture for the cover. They ended up sketching a picture of me, which was the only sketch of the winner in the history of this award.

Needless to say, the article was extremely complimentary about our company and our family. Included were some generous comments from longtime friends and associates in the industry, people such as Phil Barach, chairman of U.S. Shoe; Jerry Miller of Shoe Biz; and Joe Famolare, the great footwear entrepreneur and showman.

Looking back on it, I think I was kind of a jerk about not cooperating with *Footwear News*, and I regret that.

In 2005, our company won *Footwear News*'s Retailer of the Year award. My son Pete accepted the award on behalf of Nordstrom. Unlike his dad, he was gracious enough to attend the ceremonies, where he told the audience, "I'm here to give a mea culpa from my dad to the industry for not coming to New York to accept the Man of the Year award in 1987."

Phil Barach was chairman and chief executive officer of U.S. Shoe Corporation for many years, and did business with our company over a long period.

In 1988, Nordstrom held a black-tie affair to celebrate the opening of Tysons Corner. Bruce was in a great mood. In front of a lot of our U.S. Shoe executives, he asked me who I thought Nordstrom's biggest vendor was.

I said, "Jones Apparel?"

"No."

"Estée Lauder?"

"No."

Bruce said, "You are our biggest vendor."

I was very surprised. Then he asked me why I thought U.S. Shoe was their biggest vendor.

"Because we make more money for you?"

"No."

"We deliver promptly and have a big reorder capability to turn your inventory?"

"No."

"Our brands are well accepted and the consumers like them?"

"No."

Bruce shook his head and said, "I thought you were a smart guy, Phil. You're our number one vendor because your tongue is always hanging out for an order. You always want to do more business. I tell my people, everything being equal, we should give U.S. Shoe a break to reward their great desire to do business. We tell our salespeople that they have to take the same attitude toward every Nordstrom customer."

When I came back to our headquarters in Cincinnati, I said to my people, "There's a lot to be learned from what Bruce said." In the end, it's the attitude of wanting to do more business: effort, effort, effort. That underscored for me the Nordstrom way of doing business.

CHAPTER 21

A NEW FLAGSHIP STORE IN OUR HOMETOWN

In the 1990s, downtown Seattle was going through a crisis. At the same time, we were thinking seriously about the future of our downtown flagship store.

Frederick & Nelson, which was the grande dame of Seattle department stores, had officially closed its doors in 1992, after 102 years, leaving an 850,000-square-foot building completely empty for several years afterward. You just can't have a building that size sitting there idle and expect to still have a thriving downtown. As the Frederick's property sat empty, it was disintegrating before our eyes. The façade was filthy, trash filled the doorways, graffiti was everywhere, and homeless people were sleeping in front of the number one retail location in town.

In the meantime, we had been discussing, internally, the future of our existing flagship store. It had served us well but was a very inefficient 245,000 square feet — three different buildings patched together, with a lot of unusable space. Customers who came to Seattle on vacation to see the Nordstrom flagship store were disappointed. But I don't think the citizens of Seattle cared very much. They were used to it.

Looking to the future, we knew there was going to come a time when we should have a flagship store that looked like a flagship store.

Downtown Seattle wasn't safe for our people who worked in the store and at our headquarters. My cousin Jim felt strongly that if downtown

Looking to the future, we knew there was going to come a time when we should have a flagship store that looked like a flagship store.

The downtown Seattle flagship store

Frederick & Nelson in the late 1940s

Seattle continued to deteriorate, we should look at moving everything to Bellevue. At that time, in the mid-1990s, business had leveled off. We had been gaining in all our other stores, but not the downtown store.

If we chose to stay in downtown Seattle, the Frederick's building would be the obvious choice, but it came with several negatives. First of all, the costs to occupy a renovated Frederick's building (which was built in 1918 and expanded in 1952) would be significantly higher than the costs of our existing store, so we would have to do a more meaningful amount of business just to break even. We had just a ballpark figure of what it might cost us to do the renovation of this one store: about $100 million. For the same amount of money, we could have built at least three suburban stores.

One of the biggest of those negatives was that in 1990, the City of Seattle, in its infinite wisdom, had closed Pine Street to vehicular traffic between Fourth and Fifth Avenues in order to make Westlake Park more friendly to foot traffic. As a result, shoppers driving west on Pine Street were diverted off Pine and away from the retail core.

We made it known that keeping Pine Street closed to car traffic was a deal breaker. I give my cousin John most of the credit on that because the rest of us were willing to go along with keeping the street closed. But John was a bulldog on that subject. He had researched every single city that had closed streets to vehicular traffic — including Tacoma, Fresno, Sacramento — and found that every single one of the retail centers had died. John showed his findings to the members of the Seattle City Council, but most of them were unmoved. He felt so strongly that this was such a gamble for us, we couldn't leave any stone unturned to get the best possible conditions and terms. There was no question that when Pine Street was closed, the traffic flow was severely hampered. When it was open, the city had the best of all worlds: the free flow of pedestrian traffic, which is able to co-exist with vehicle traffic.

On March 14, 1995, the people of Seattle voted on whether to reopen the one block of Pine Street to vehicular traffic. People knew that a yes vote would clear the way for the development of our store and other projects. By a vote of 61 percent to 39 percent, the reopening was approved.

This deal had several moving parts. Matt Griffin, a local developer, was interested in developing the block that occupied the parking garage across from Frederick's on Sixth Avenue, between Pine and Olive Streets. Crucial to his plans was developing the Frederick's building. Griffin and his company, Pine Street Associates, realized that developing both the Frederick's building and the parking garage was going to be too much for them, so a trade was conceived. Pine Street Associates bought the Frederick & Nelson building, then swapped it to us for the rights to the

Our decision to move into the Frederick & Nelson space set everything in motion to rescue downtown Seattle.

old Nordstrom site, which they would redevelop. Pine Street Associates then went ahead with building Pacific Place, a vertical retail mall, over the site of the old parking garage, which was completely rebuilt and is now the finest parking facility in downtown Seattle.

I give credit to Norm Rice, who was then the mayor of Seattle, for his leadership. He formed a public–private partnership, which turned into probably the best financial investment the city of Seattle has ever made in its downtown. Norm Rice was a great example of a progressive politician, similar to Neil Goldschmidt, the former mayor of Portland, who persuaded us to move our Portland store across the street to a bigger space — at a time when we were thinking about moving entirely out of Portland.

Our decision to move into the Frederick & Nelson space set everything in motion to rescue downtown Seattle. At that same time, Jim Ellis, one of the great citizens in the history of Seattle, was leading the charge for building the expansion of the Washington State Convention & Trade Center. Jim has said that our decision to move to the Frederick's site was the catalyst for building the new addition, which effectively doubled the available event space. The Convention Center is located over Interstate 5, just a couple of blocks from our store.

On August 21, 1998, we officially opened our new 383,000-square-foot flagship store, which also houses our corporate headquarters and Washington regional offices.

When Frederick's was in business, they used about 850,000 square feet of retail space and, in their best year, recorded about $40 million in sales. By comparison, in our first year in that building, we did more than $100 million in sales, using less than half the selling space.

But it was a gamble because we didn't know if we could do enough

It's true that there was a civic element to our decision, as well as emotional and financial elements.

business there. Just a few years earlier, we had undergone a major expansion at our Bellevue Square store, bringing it up to about 285,000 square feet. Today, our downtown and Bellevue Square stores are running neck and neck in sales volume in the chain and gaining on South Coast Plaza, which is number one.

Some people have suggested that we moved to the Frederick & Nelson space because this is our hometown, and it's true that there was a civic element to our decision, as well as emotional and financial elements. Anybody who knows me, or knows our family, understands that we're Seattle first. We feel it here in the heart. I was raised doing my back-to-school shopping with my mother at Frederick's, so this building had a very important place in our hearts. But when you're running a public company, you're committed to your shareholders, so you have to balance the heart with the head. I don't think this building would have worked for a retailer from out of town, but it worked for us. I take great pride in this store, which is a beautiful flagship building, our corporate headquarters, in the best location in our hometown, which has one of the most vibrant downtowns in the United States. We like to think we did our part to make that a reality.

REINVEST IN YOUR STORES

As our stores age, they should be remodeled so that we retain our contemporary, fashionable image. No frayed carpets and chipped paint.

We have discovered over the years that when we do a major remodel in stores, it initially creates more business. People are curious to see what's going on, and are attracted to "Men Working" signs, sawhorses, and Visqueen coverings. Now, that's a big change from the way I was raised, when my dad and uncles wanted to squeeze one more year out of everything. If someone said, "Gee, I need a new wrap desk," their answer was: "One more year." If there was a rip in the carpet, Elmer would tape it down with duct tape and say, "That'll do it for one more year."

Back in the early days, we weren't a fancy store, so nobody marked us down for doing that. If we did that today, it would be wrong. No more duct tape.

GOOD COMPETITION MAKES US BETTER

Mall developers tell us that we have become the most sought-after anchor tenant, a reality that has greatly helped our expansion plans. These developers, who understand us better than anybody, like us because we do more sales per square foot, which means that we build more business for their development. At one time, our annual sales per square foot was better than any of our competitors', but today that distinction belongs to Neiman's. On the other hand, because our stores are so much bigger than theirs, it's difficult to make a direct comparison between us. But when you compare us to all of Federated Department Stores (which today has 850 stores, compared to our 100 full-line stores, 51 Rack stores, five Façonnable boutiques, and two Jeffrey boutiques), we do much more per square foot.

When we go into shopping centers all over the country, we are an anchor store. Anchors can drive very interesting agreements. The competition can have clauses giving them approval rights for any other anchor that could be added to the shopping center. We almost never get approved. I honestly think that we bring business to those shopping malls because when you create traffic, everyone benefits. We want to be near Neiman's, which is our number one competitor in designer women's apparel. They do some things better than we do, but we do some things better than they do. Between the two of us, we'll compete and we'll create a lot of business.

Of all the different groups of people that I've known through my life, the most interesting and fascinating are the developers. The senior Simon Brothers and Al Taubman are great characters — smart as a whip and good salesmen. You could write novels about these gutsy guys, who rolled the dice and let it all hang out.

One of the most extraordinary families that we have ever known are the Ghermezian brothers — Eskandar, Nader, Raphael, and Bahman — who emigrated from Iran to Canada. They had the courage and audacity to build the world's largest shopping center in, of all places, Edmonton, Alberta. The 5.3-million-square-foot West Edmonton Mall has become a destination for shoppers from all over the world.

We first came in contact with them when they were building Mall of America in Minnesota, the largest center in the United States. We are pretty conservative, but they talked us into joining their project because we were so impressed with the gall of it all. We had never met such unusual businessmen, who had the vision, the courage, and the means to carry it out. Like us Nordstroms, the Ghermezians operated as a family unit, and if you dealt with one Ghermezian, you dealt with them all. My son Erik was the first manager of our Mall of America store, which has been one of our most successful units.

Early on in our expansion, we thought we were wringing every cent we could get out of those developers. But as I get older, I'm convinced that the Macy's of the world and some of the other sharp guys were getting what we got; probably more. They were the biggest, but we tended to perform better than most.

Nowadays, unfortunately, a lot of developers are bound to their computers and the numbers, and less to the gut than these great characters I grew up with. Ernie Hahn was another good example. For years, the Hahn Company developed more malls for us than any other developer.

Ernie was a wonderful man, but I remember negotiating with him, and he would cry, "You guys are taking every cent I own." Some time later, however, when I visited him at his home down in Rancho Santa Fe, I saw that he had several golf holes on his property. I said, "Ernie, I have this little house on Mercer Island, and you have this huge estate. I'm never going to believe what you tell me."

John Whitacre with his initial leadership team. Front row, from left:
Blake and Bill Nordstrom. Back row, from left: Pete and Dan
Nordstrom, John Whitacre, Erik and Jim A. Nordstrom.

We learned what can happen if we get away from our culture.

CHAPTER 22

CHANGING OF THE GUARD (AGAIN)

Throughout the 1970s and most of the 1980s, we were a retail juggernaut. But toward the end of the 1980s, our business started to plateau. It wasn't dramatic, but you could see the signs.

What happened? Well, the buck stops with John, Jim, Jack, and me. Frankly, we didn't do as good a job in the last seven or eight years as we did in the first 25 years because we took our eye off the ball and didn't work as hard. Our business was doing well, and we were thinking, "Gee, I can take one more day off a week and the business still does great." We felt we had earned it, so we became interested in other things and took our focus off the business. We were all guilty of that; I am as critical of myself as I am of all of us. The fact is, the four of us weren't on the same page as much as we had always been in the past.

In 1991, we were all still relatively young. I was 58, John was 54, Jim was 52, and Jack was 60. But in terms of retail, which is a young person's game, we were getting long in the tooth. We needed more energy because retail is energy. Our grandpa had retired at 58, and our uncles had retired in their sixties, turning over the reins to us young guys. (My dad actually retired once when he was 50, but his retirement lasted only half a year. It was football season and he got to see all the Husky games. When the season was over, he came back, thank goodness.)

Our team decided to shake things up a bit. We had realized that when you know every side of every issue, it drives you to inaction.

We thought the best way to strengthen our top management would be to take four of our best executives, make them co-presidents, creating an Office of the President, and see what happened. We made the announcement at our annual shareholders meeting in May 1991. The four people we selected were John Whitacre, Ray Johnson, Darrel Hume, and Galen Jefferson. John, Jim, Jack, and I were co-chairmen of the board, and Bob Bender was named vice chairman.

In 1992 and 1993, our performance was disappointing. We just didn't do the transition right, perhaps because we weren't as close to the business as we used to be. Darrel and Galen stepped down, leaving Whitacre and Johnson as co-presidents.

We thought that John and Ray could be a pretty good team. Both of them had been with our company for many, many years.

John Whitacre had started with us as a shoe salesman when he was an undergraduate at the UW, where he played offensive tackle on the Husky football team, and eventually managed our stores in Tacoma, Bellevue Square, and Walnut Creek, California. In 1988, we entrusted the opening of our first East Coast store, Tysons Corner Center, to John, who did a terrific job of planting the seeds of our culture in another part of the country.

Ray Johnson and Bob Bender were the only high-ranking executives that we had hired from another retailer. Before joining our team in 1969, Ray worked in personnel at The Bon Marché. Soon after we hired him to do personnel for us, it became obvious that he was a retailer. He eventually managed our stores in Bellevue Square and downtown Seattle, became general manager of our Washington/Alaska region, and then was appointed general manager of Northern California in 1985. During Ray's tenure in Northern California, we built 12 stores in six years.

Today, even though he has retired from day-to-day responsibilities, Ray still does special assignments for us. He often goes to recognition meetings around the country, spends time talking to store managers, and then comes back and reports his impressions to Erik, who is the president of full-line stores. Ray, who is one of us, understands our unique culture and is able to look at things with a different set of eyes, which is invaluable.

VEERING OFF OUR PATH

John and Ray worked well together as a team for three years, and things started to turn around. When Ray retired at the end of 1996, we thought that Whitacre was doing great, so we let him continue on his own. Unfortunately, John took a path that we weren't on. What he did was well intended, but business was soft and he felt pressure to do something to turn things around.

John had other issues to think about as well. Coming up in the organization was the next generation of Nordstroms — seven smart, capable, hardworking guys in their twenties and early thirties who were full of energy and ambition. Six of them were named to the Office of the President. My generation had taken over when we were about that age, but this was now a much bigger, more complicated business. Clearly, this generation was not yet ready to take the reins.

In hindsight, it's clear that Whitacre was in a difficult position. In his desire to be successful and move the company forward, he took a path that shifted the company away from the culture he had been raised in. I take the blame for a lot of that. As directors, John, Jack, and I could have interceded more to help find solutions. We should have been on our toes.

There were some really poor initiatives, particularly an advertising campaign in early 2000 called "Reinvent yourself," which focused on trendy styles but resulted in alienating many of our longtime customers. I can't tell you how much mail I got from customers, who wrote: "You're telling me I have to reinvent myself. You go reinvent yourself."

We have always realized that when you're trying to appeal to a broad cross section of customers, you have to walk a fine line. You want to be current and fashionable in order to appeal to a younger customer, who will grow with you, but you don't want to be so cutting-edge that you leave behind the people who built your business for you.

During this period, every facet of our business was being altered in ways that we felt were hurtful and were going to take us down.

My cousin Jim died of prostate cancer in 1996, at the age of 56. His untimely death was a blow to all of us because Jim was a one-of-a-kind man who loved this company and was loved by everyone. Nobody ever had more friends than Jim. He was very strong-minded about the culture and about doing things a certain way.

Jim's death was a catalyst for addressing our problems. We had a fragmentation of direction, which is what you don't want with a

We have always realized that when you're trying to appeal to a broad cross section of customers, you have to walk a fine line.

committee or group. You can have a difference of opinion, but you can't go in different directions.

Business was wildly inconsistent. Net earnings went from $140.8 million in 1993 to $202.5 million in 1994, then back down to $146.3 million in 1996. We reached $206.7 million in 1998, only to fall back to $101.9 million in 2000.

Wall Street and Main Street were both disappointed in us. The opinion of the media was summed up in a *Time* magazine article on us that had the headline "Nordstrom Loses Its Luster" and a color photograph of a crushed Nordstrom gift box wrapped in tattered ribbon. This and similar stinging stories in *The New York Times*, *The Wall Street Journal*, and *Women's Wear Daily* questioned whether Whitacre and the new generation of Nordstroms were up to the task.

During this difficult time, those of us in the third generation thought we might lose this business. It was in enough trouble that somebody could have come in from the outside and bought it. In those days, our family owned such a significant percentage of the stock that a corporate raider would have had a very difficult time attacking our company, but might have been able to pull it off. My family and I were never going to be poor; somebody was going to pay us for our stock. But we were afraid that our reputation, our status, our accomplishments were going to go out the window.

John Whitacre understood that it was necessary to produce numbers maybe better than we did right at that moment because he knew he was in the hot seat. At some point, he concluded that he was going to have to run the business in a different way, and he selected some people to be leaders of this business who, in our judgment, were not the right people. He brought in several outsiders and put them in key upper-manage-

The change of course was well intended, but it was the wrong course.

ment positions. The change of course was well intended, but it was the wrong course.

He began bringing in a lot of consultants. Now, there's nothing wrong with consultants for specialized parts of the business such as IT or receiving and marking. But selling shoes? No sir. Don't tell us how to do that.

I'd walk around and see all these strange faces, all these consultants roaming around our company. One day I asked Whitacre, "Would anybody come to me if I hung up a shingle that said 'Bruce Nordstrom, retail consultant'?"

He said, "Oh, Mr. Bruce, they'd be lined up to speak to you."

I said, "Well, I'm right here. You've never asked me, and I don't cost you a dime."

He didn't have an answer to that, which I think embarrassed him. John was an "aw-shucks" kind of guy, which is my kind of guy, but he never asked for advice. Had he come into my office or John Nordstrom's office or Jack McMillan's office and said, "I'm struggling with this assignment and I need some help on how best to proceed," we might have figured out a way to get through this period.

Some of us Nordstroms felt that we had been left out in the cold. And we were the major shareholders. Whitacre didn't want to fire any of the fourth generation, but what he did was emasculate some of them, effectively sending them a message that some of the guys were on his team and some of the guys were not on his team.

As things got bad, I think he panicked, and took a different track from the one that got us here. Perhaps, given a lot more time and money, he might have succeeded, but it sure wouldn't be the same business.

It was a confusing time for our board, which had to deal with the Nordstrom contingent on one side and the Whitacre team on the other. They were trying to support Whitacre because he was the chairman. Our reputation was still relatively untarnished, but our numbers told us that that was not going to last very long.

John, Jack, and I were the first ones to raise the flag. We went to the board and told them that we were losing the culture of this business, and we blamed ourselves because we were the ones who had picked this team and devised the game plan, which clearly wasn't working.

Finally, on August 31, 2000, Whitacre resigned, after 24 years with our company, as did Michael Stein, our chief financial officer.

After undergoing a national search for candidates from outside the company, our board named Blake, then 39, to be president. Blake had been president of Nordstrom Rack Group, and had been one of the co-presidents until that post was eliminated earlier in 2000. I accepted the board's request for me to return as its chairman. A few days after Blake became president, Pete was named president of our full-line stores; he is now president of merchandising. Soon after, Erik was named executive vice president of full-line stores; he was later elevated to president of stores.

Blake had had the least recognition from Whitacre, and the lowest-profile job, of any of the Nordstroms in the fourth generation. He occupied a tiny, windowless office in the Nordstrom Rack on Second Avenue in downtown Seattle, where I would visit him every once in a while.

Initially, Wall Street was unimpressed by the elevation of another family member to the top position. One so-called "expert" actually said: "I don't see this as much of a change. [Blake] talked about customer service and about listening to customers, the same platitudes we have heard before." But it was those so-called "platitudes" that made Nordstrom Nordstrom.

We promoted Mike Koppel to CFO. Like Allan and John Goesling, the father-son team who together were our CFOs for 50 years, Mike brought to the job an understanding that nothing happens in our company until someone sells something. He became a key player in helping the company achieve outstanding results.

John Whitacre later became CEO of Harrod's in London, a job he held for a couple of years before returning to Seattle in 2002. Sadly, in November of that year, he died of a heart attack at age 50.

Having to part company with John Whitacre was the single biggest disappointment I've had in this business. It was my job to tell him in a one-on-one meeting, which was one of the toughest things I ever had to do because John was a wonderful, likable man who was perhaps the hardest worker I ever saw (and I've seen a lot of hard workers). Like everyone else who knew him, I thought the world of John Whitacre, who was as much Nordstrom as any of us. He rose from the selling floor through every kind of job in our company all the way to the top. Our service ethic was embedded in him from the day he arrived at Nordstrom until the day he left.

When I think about what happened, I'm saddened and baffled. It was a tough load for John and his people to deal with 10 Nordstroms (of the third and fourth generations) who were not all on the same page. I'm not critical of those who were on a different page because they were earnest and well intended and hardworking. I'm not sure anyone could have made this situation work.

On the positive side, we were heartened to find that our culture, which had helped us build the business and gave us our success, was not in shambles yet, but showing signs of weakening. The strength of our culture enabled us to weather the challenges we faced. I'm a big believer that people's spirits are much better when they're on a winning team. When the team loses, spirits go down. We were losing, and yet when I visited our stores, I saw our people smiling and giving good service — as good as they could. There were some rumblings of "Why don't you get us better stuff," but I didn't get a lot of bad service letters; I did receive a lot of bad merchandise letters.

Setbacks are sobering, but occasionally they are good for you. In hindsight, going through that troubled period was a valuable experience for this company because it knocked right out the window any thought of being a juggernaut. We learned what can happen if we get away from our culture.

The strength of our culture enabled us to weather the challenges we faced.

THE ROLE OF THE BOARD

During this period, we learned to more highly value our board of directors. When we became a public company, the first quality we looked for in a director was compatibility. The second quality was respect — would that director reflect well on our company? When called upon, would he or she offer an honest and true opinion about what we were doing? Having retail experience was not the most important criterion. We wanted our directors to bring something unique to the table. Over the years, we have had some outstanding directors who have helped us steer this company on the right course.

The relationship between directors and officers of public companies has changed since President George W. Bush signed the Sarbanes-Oxley Act. This legislative response to several major corporate and accounting scandals has brought about greater scrutiny of the role and responsibilities of directors, who are compelled to look at every phase of the business with a much more critical eye than in years past, when directors were generally more supportive. It's a difficult atmosphere, but it's essential for the long-term health of the company.

THE FOURTH GENERATION

As our organization became realigned, several members of the fourth generation of Nordstroms left the company to pursue other interests. My cousin John's son Jim A. Nordstrom left when Whitacre was taking the company in a direction that he was not comfortable with. My cousin Jim's sons Bill and Dan also left, Bill shortly before Whitacre did and Dan about a year and a half later.

While they respected one another, the fourth generation didn't have the kind of closeness of thought that our generation had. When some of them decided to leave, there were no bad feelings. They were in a position to do other things, which is what they are doing now, and they are very happy. They are all hardworking guys, and I greatly respect each and every one of them. I will always wonder how different it might have been if my cousin Jim were still alive. He was a terrific leader. It's hard to know how he would have felt and what role he could have possibly played. In any case, I give them all credit for sticking to it and getting their jobs done through a difficult time.

I do want to thank Dan and the team he put together in his last assignment with us, as president of Nordstrom Direct, which is our Internet and catalog business. Dan essentially started our Direct division, which was first a catalog business, and later played a key role in building Nordstrom.com. When Dan left, his right arm, Jim Bromley, took over and did a great job growing the business. Today, my cousin Jim's fourth son, Jamie, who has been working for the company his whole professional life, is president of Nordstrom Direct. The basic foundation laid by Dan has served us well, and Jamie and his team are doing an outstanding job working toward our goal of being a complete multi-channel retailer. I know that Jim would be smiling.

BALANCING FAMILY AND SHAREHOLDER INTERESTS

As family companies — even public companies — grow, the great challenge is how to balance the interests of the family and the interests of the shareholders. We are one of the few large corporations in this country, and the only national retailer, run by the fourth generation of the founding family. The few remaining famous family retailers are not the factors they once were. Certain retail families leave a longer-lasting imprint on their corporate cultures; at Neiman Marcus, the influence of Stanley Marcus, who passed away several years ago, continues to this day.

Over the years, we've interfaced with a number of family-business experts, but I thought the advice they gave us was pabulum, obvious stuff. For example, they tell you that you've got to have a meeting and "agree to agree." We already do that.

Some members of our family have wanted to do other things, and God bless them, it's their stock, they can do with it whatever they like.

We take the long-term view because it's our name and reputation that we want to protect and enhance. Taking the long-term view isn't as easy as it used to be because our family doesn't own as large a percentage of stock as we once did. Nevertheless, today our family is still the largest shareholder.

Our board currently doesn't want an Office of the President, even though that is the way Everett, Elmer, and Lloyd ran it, and the way John, Jim, Jack, and I ran it. To date, the board has supported a more conventional structure of having one person serve as president. As it so happens, Blake is a good choice for that. He's got a motor that burns as fast as anybody's I've ever seen. Pete and Erik, who are both extremely talented in their own right, are willing to defer the title to Blake, knowing that their brother doesn't make a move without talking to them. It's a credit to the three of them that they're able to work together so closely and utilize the strengths of each guy. I think the board recognizes the validity of our unique culture and our historical way of doing things.

In today's corporate climate, directors and management are under the microscope at all times, so we have no illusions; we have to have good numbers. As Al Davis, owner of the Oakland Raiders, is famous for saying, "Just win, baby."

THE TURNAROUND

I believe that good leaders must be good listeners. After Blake was named president, Erik and I went around the country to talk to our salespeople, which was a tempering experience. We specifically said at the beginning of each of those meetings that we were there to learn from their point of view because this company was not performing as it had in the past. What was it going to take to get us back to where we were? We asked for criticism and we got it, but it was positive criticism from loyal employees, who told us that morale was down because the merchandise in the stores wasn't right. The merchandise is their ammunition; it's how they make their living. "Give us some ammunition that's right, out here on the sales floor, and we'll show you something," they told us. "We'll give you some numbers that you can really be proud of."

We did, they sold it, and the rest, as they say, is history. The experience of listening to our people helped this company more than anything else we could have done. Ask your top people what they need, because they have answers.

We take the long-term view because it's our name and reputation that we want to protect and enhance.

My cousin Jim Nordstrom was a loyal friend, loyal to the family, hardworking, and a bit of a cutup, with dancing eyes. I once took care of him when Kitty and Elmer went to Europe, and he was a test of my responsibility.

Over the years, we just had more fun and more laughs, and very good, deep conversations. He would say to me, "Don't ever tell me anything you don't want me to tell other people. I just can't keep a secret."

Everybody loved Jim. Everybody had funny stories to tell about him. He might get people mad at him every once in a while, but every friend of his knew that if they needed something, they could call Jim and he would do it. I asked him to take Wayne to the Masters golf tournament for Wayne's 60th birthday, and Jim didn't hesitate. It was the best experience that Wayne had ever had, and he talks about it to this day.

Jim died with more dignity than almost anybody I know. When he learned that he had cancer, I was in his office, and he talked about it in a very accepting way. I was in awe of his maturity and honesty. It was amazing. His son Jamie is so much like Jim.

If Jim came back today and saw everything this company has become, he would be proud and amazed. He'd be critical of some things and speak his mind. But he would be proud and amazed.

Charlie has led many large corporations, including DHL Airways, Inc., and the Fresh Choice restaurant chain. Before he became a Nordstrom director in the 1980s, he was a Nordstrom vendor.

In the 1960s, I was working for the DuPont Company. We had a new synthetic footwear product, and we had plans to take it to the couture level. Somebody told me, "If you're going to sell to retailers, you've got to get out to Nordstrom." I said, "Who?" They told me Nordstrom was the number one footwear store in the country.

I called somebody at Nordstrom to set up an appointment, and then flew out to Seattle with my samples of shoes made in this synthetic product. I thought they were going to send me to some junior buyer. Instead, I walked into a room and all the Nordstroms were there. The reception just blew me away because they didn't know me at all. But they couldn't have treated me better. That was the way they handled their vendors, with respect, which is why their vendors love 'em. I came back raving about Nordstrom. Eventually, Nordstrom carried the product in their store.

Years later, Jim Nordstrom asked me to become a director. At the same time, I had been asked to go on the board of The Gap, but I chose the Nordstrom board because I was so impressed with the Nordstrom way.

I became close to Blake and was a big fan of his. I used to visit with him a lot when he managed the Hillsdale store. I was impressed as hell with his commitment, focus, attitude, and the way he conducted himself. One of the good things about Blake was that he knew what he didn't know. He didn't have the attitude that he was a Nordstrom and therefore knew everything. He was very open in his desire to improve.

In the late 1990s, when we had to make a management change, any board member who knew the Nordstrom culture knew that we could never bring in someone from the outside. We had the talent inside. Thank God that Bruce was willing to devote his time to be there, to be a mentor for that whole group, and maintain the continuity that was needed.

ALFRED E. OSBORNE JR., PH.D.

Al Osborne became a director in 1987 and served for 19 years, retiring in 2006. Al, who is Senior Associate Dean of the UCLA Anderson Graduate School of Management, was our first African-American board member.

In the late 1990s, the biggest challenge the Nordstrom board faced was how to restore the luster and build the leadership of the company for the future. You could see that going outside for a CEO was not an option. An outside CEO would have wanted the job valued very differently than someone from the inside. Therefore, it would have been destructive to the collaborative management style that exists at the top of the company.

Who could we trust with what Nordstrom was? In the end, the only people you could trust were the ones whose name was on the door. It was important that our customers saw that a Nordstrom was at the helm.

We wanted one member of the fourth generation to step up and be more equal than everybody else. Blake had the presence and skills to be that person, although at the time, his skills were unpolished. I knew all along that Blake was the natural leader of the three, and Pete and Erik were also developing their own management-leadership styles. Still, there was a feeling that this was too much to dump on Blake right away.

At the same time, the board had a lot of confidence in Rick Hernandez, who was relatively new to the board but a quick study. Rick has emerged as a mentor to Blake, and is now the non-executive chairman of the board.

The other part of the deal was asking Bruce to come back to take a more active role as chairman. We thought that Bruce could anchor Blake in a formal way and stabilize the company, and Rick could broaden Blake's perspective as a senior executive.

I would call the decision [to promote Blake to president] courageous but calculated. In retrospect, it was what we should have done in any event. Nordstrom is like the swoosh of the Nike logo — when you see Nordstrom, you know what it stands for.

Salespeople can access Nordstrom.com to find merchandise for their customers.

Since we're open to fashion, we should be open to technology.

CHAPTER 23

CHANGING WITH THE TIMES

In the old days, the decisions that affected each store were made at the store level, not at headquarters. When we were just running shoe stores, the store manager did the buying; it was his inventory; it was his baby.

For the longest time, I felt that a buyer had to be on the floor all the time, in order to hear what the customer was asking for that we didn't have. No computer in the world can tell you that. I still feel that our best buyers, merchandise managers, and department managers must periodically get to the floor to ask the salespeople, "What did that customer want that we didn't have?" If management reacts quickly to their recommendations, that really solidifies both the salesperson's and the customer's loyalty.

As we've gotten bigger, our company has, by necessity, become less decentralized. As we moved geographically and the numbers got bigger, we had to find a better way to get our arms around the business. We had to have our best people doing that.

My cousin Jim and I were the last of the Mohicans as far as thinking that we never wanted to centralize this business. As a result, we probably hung on to that notion a little too long. I had to be sold on technology because I felt that the decisions had to be made by the people who were actually on the firing line. There was no technology that could tell you exactly how to make your decisions. In the old days, at the end of every day the manager would have each salesman turn in the list of the things he had sold, then compile them in a book. It was all done by hand. But in the late 1960s and early '70s, we were getting to the size where that couldn't work.

My attitude toward technology gradually became more benign. Since we're open to fashion, we should be open to technology. Over the past couple of years, we have spent nearly $300 million on IT systems that have helped us to control our inventory, connect with our customers, and serve them better. Technology also assists our salespeople. If their store is out of stock in a particular item in a certain size or color, they can use our inventory-management system to locate that item in one of our other stores.

This is how the interior of the Second Avenue store looked around 1910.

Today, we're on the cutting edge of technology and we're also doing better. The money we've spent on technology has been worth it. Is technology the reason for our better performance? I think it is a reason but not *the* reason. Technology is a tool that we use, but it is not, by itself, the reason. We are turning our inventory a lot better now, which means that we make more money while operating on better margins. One of the benefits of better inventory control is that we can build stores a little smaller because we can have more selling space and less back space. We have just as much selling space as we used to have, but 20,000 or 30,000 less feet total space.

Today, our buying is regionally decentralized, which is a nice middle ground. Pete Nordstrom, who is in charge of merchandising, has revamped the buying structure. For a few years, he had 15 direct reports, which was way too many, and it's now been reduced to eight. Because we have stores all over the country, weather makes a big difference in what we buy, so we need to have people in the regions making those decisions.

In general, my sons face the same challenges that we did, but the numbers are bigger. The main difference is that when I was in my forties, I was still pretty close to the sales floor. They are pretty close for an $8 billion business, but not as close as we once were. On the other hand, they have a lot more information at their fingertips than I ever had, and they are smart enough to use it.

I admit that I also dragged my feet on Internet shopping. When we first started thinking about at-home shopping, I said that since our point of difference is the way we treat people, how could we do that over the phone or on the Internet? But today I'm a believer. The people at Nordstrom.com and our call centers are true Nordies who understand what we're trying to do and who do a darn good job.

One of our newest design concepts is shown here in the interior of the NorthPark shoe department in Dallas.

With my sons, Blake, Erik, and Pete, in 2005

If there is a key to our success so far, it is that we've been able to retain that **entrepreneurial feeling** in an $8 billion company.

CHAPTER 24

LOOKING BACK, LOOKING FORWARD

There have been so many dramatic changes in retail since the time I started earning money working in our shoe store. When I was a young man, there were many great regional department stores — Frederick & Nelson, Rich's, Dayton's, Meier & Frank — the list goes on and on. The problem for those stores was that, as the first generation left the business, there was generally a dramatic falloff and a lack of appreciation for what it was that got them there. There was also, in many cases, a lack of business acumen. Eventually, those stores disappeared.

After all the mergers and acquisitions, there is now no such thing as a large local independent department store. We are as close as it gets, and even though we are a large specialty store (carrying shoes, apparel, cosmetics, and accessories, but not hard goods) in 27 states, we try to be responsive to each region we are in.

In all fairness to the large retailers, they are better businesspeople than most of the people they are absorbing, and some of them are darn good merchants. But it's extremely challenging to acquire a company and then try to apply your culture to theirs.

Department stores will continue to be our single major competition. The good news is that, for the most part, the delineation between them and us is very clear as far as service goes. As long as that's true, we've got a chance. The bigger they get, the harder it is for them to give good service.

Many department stores have a growing number of departments that they don't actually run; they lease them out to the vendors, who run the department. That doesn't happen here, and it represents a significant difference.

Many big retailers are guilty of being run by accountants rather than by merchants. One exception is Federated Department Stores, a holding company that includes more than 850 stores, which does have a real merchant as CEO. Nevertheless, they have to place so much emphasis on squeezing the expenses and trying to deliver the bottom line. For most companies in our industry, the number one operating cost is selling; salespeople represent the biggest single expense a retailer has. Consequently, any accountant worth his or her salt is going to look at that line first and think, "Gee, if we cut 10 percent of the help, that 10 percent is going to go right to the bottom line." No it's not. The customer doesn't get helped, and the store loses sales. Sales are the deal. Sales is how you become successful. Our selling cost, I would guess, is the highest of any retailer I know, but we have a pretty good bottom line.

As we go from town to town, our toughest competition in many ways is the mom-and-pop stores — not in volume, of course, but in their ability to win the hearts of their customers. The little guys have a better entrepreneurial spirit than the big guys because they have to give it their all every day. If there is a key to our success so far, it is that we've been able to retain that entrepreneurial feeling in an $8 billion company. That's pretty unusual.

VENDORS

Vendors have always been important to us, and we often feel beholden to them. I know enough about other companies and how they treat vendors to tell you that this is not the norm.

Given today's consolidation in our industry, we have tried to enhance our dealings with our vendors. While most major stores carry the same lines that we do, we are quicker at identifying small up-and-coming vendors, which was one of the hallmarks of Neiman's success. They could spot designers and manufacturers who were just getting started but who had a great idea that no one else had. That's happening less and less in the industry.

Some retailers forbid their buyers to buy from any resource that isn't on their "matrix," which often is determined by financial or operational criteria. But what is the customer interested in? What might the customer be interested in?

Many big retailers are guilty of being run by accountants rather than by merchants.

One of the things that we as a company have to keep striving for is to recognize the up-and-comer, the person who doesn't have a lot of experience but who has good ideas.

In 1992, when we were established as one of America's top retailers, we created the Partners In Excellence Award, which gives public recognition to those vendors who demonstrate a commitment to quality, value, service, partnership, and business ethics. I don't remember how it started. There was no flash of light. We just felt that publicly acknowledging the best vendors would be tremendously rewarding for them.

We honor them at our annual shareholders meeting, where we talk about our relationship with the vendors and how they have done some amazing things for us. They have treated us like special customers, and we return the compliment. We are not spouting platitudes; we are expressing how we feel. It's emotional for them and it's emotional for us.

We've had an interesting universe of vendors who have been our partners over the years. I remember when we were trying to persuade Polo Ralph Lauren Corporation to ship to us more regularly and (to our way of thinking) more fairly, because we felt we were the last people in the country that they were sending orders to. The person servicing our account suggested that we express our concern directly to Ralph.

We were told that Ralph would be coming to Seattle soon, and it might be nice for us to play tennis with him at the Seattle Tennis Club, where one of our family was a member. We were also told that Ralph was an A-minus tennis player, so Jim, John, and I practiced like crazy because we didn't want to embarrass ourselves.

On the day of the game Ralph arrived, his clothing brand new and sparkling. We started to play doubles, and it soon became obvious that if Ralph was an A-minus player, then we were A-plus. Our competitive juices started flowing. We did not play tennis to ingratiate ourselves with him. John, Jim, and I all rotated playing with him, and whoever was his partner was on the losing side.

To Ralph's credit, deliveries improved from that day forward, and we became a significant customer of his company.

Ralph is the founder and CEO of what is arguably the most successful clothing manufacturer in this country. Pretty good for a kid from the Bronx whose real name is Ralph Lipschitz.

CHANGES IN THE SHOE BUSINESS

These days, the shoe business is much more difficult. When I started, and for many years afterward, vendors had their own factories, where they owned the machinery, the lasts, the patterns, and so on. I used to go into the factories and see our merchandise coming through, which is so helpful to running a successful business. For me, there's nothing like the smell of a shoe factory — the leather, cement, and dye.

Today, many big corporations own several different businesses, and most of the shoes are made offshore.

In the footwear business, there is so much money involved. You need to have some staple merchandise that has a shelf life of a year or two or three, as well as new, fresh merchandise every season to keep the ball rolling. Because of the size of their investment, a lot more people stay in the industry, and you get to know them better. Once they get their foot in the door, they are not going away.

Shoe business characters are wonderful people, and I value my experience with them. When I think of friends in this industry, I think of a guy like Phil Barach, who eventually became chairman of U.S. Shoe Corporation. Initially, it took us a while to start doing business with Phil. For many years, U.S. Shoe's leading brand was Red Cross Shoes, which it sold to a lot of other retailers in Seattle. That did not make my dad very happy, and for many years, he forbade us to do business with U.S. Shoe.

When Phil became president of the Jumping Jacks division of U.S. Shoe, we gave him a small order on a new line of girls' shoes, which was approved by Elmer. A week later, the order was canceled. My dad told Phil that he had promised the head of Stride Rite that he would not carry another line of children's shoes in our stores, so the Jumping Jacks order would have violated his handshake agreement with Stride Rite.

"You're a nice young man and I admire your persistence. We can't get rid of you," my dad told Phil. "I hate to do this, but we still won't give you an order."

Phil took the positive, long-term view that he was going to overcome that resistance, and he was right — eventually, my father relented. When I became president of the company, I called Phil and said, "My father has given me permission to do anything I want to do. One of the first things I want to do is add Red Cross shoes and other brands." Phil flew out to Seattle the next day, and over the years we did a tremendous business with him and his company.

Another of my favorite people is Joe Famolare, one of the most innovative and hardworking guys in the business. Joe is a great promoter, with more than a little bit of P. T. Barnum in him. Long before people like Ralph Lauren and Tommy Hilfiger personified their merchandise, there was Joe Famolare.

Joe was famous for his over-the-top in-store appearances. I'll never forget the time he talked me into letting him bring a traveling show of some 20 dancers and musicians from Sardinia, an island off the coast of Italy where Joe was making shoes. It was a wild scene, with everyone wearing traditional Sardinian costumes. I think a few of our salesmen ended up flirting with some of the Sardinian women.

Joe and I had a wonderful relationship, but he wanted his way all the time. I had to say no on some occasions, just on general principle. I said, "Joe, this is a two-way street."

In the early 1970s, Joe introduced the Get There shoe, a thick rubber unit sole with four waves under the toe, ball of the foot, arch, and heel. With a negative toe and a negative heel, and waves in the middle, the shoe produced a natural rocking motion when you walked. Joe's shoe anticipated the walking-shoe craze that was later popularized by brands such as Easy Spirit and Rockport. Years later, Joe gave me a sterling silver replica of that shoe, with a plaque that reads, "To Bruce Nordstrom, commemorating the millionth pair of Get There shoes. Thanks for helping me 'Get There.'"

For me, there's nothing like the smell of a shoe factory — the leather, cement, and dye.

NORDSTROM QUALITY CENTER

With the Nordstrom Quality Center, we've found another way to help our business — and to help the vendors in the process. Over the years, our biggest shoe problem was matching up the mismated ones, which was very hard to do in individual stores because, in the natural course of business, some shoes bought for one store might get transferred or returned to another store within our company. Our people used to have "Singles Parties," when the managers would spend one whole day matching up shoes in the distribution center, where many would find their "mates." It was a waste of management's time, and it became an increasingly bigger problem.

Add to that all the shoes that were worn once and then returned. We can refurbish them and then mark down these virtually new shoes and sell them at The Rack.

Blake came up with the idea of creating a facility in Tukwila, south of Seattle, that spruces up those shoes and ensures that they are suitable for selling. Today, our entire company sends its singles to Tukwila. Blake is very proud of this operation because it saves millions of dollars for our company each year.

The Nordstrom Quality Center also takes in defective shoes and clothing merchandise that can be repaired. We sort all of one vendor's merchandise into one bin, then invite the vendor's representative (or, in some cases, the principal of the company) to Tukwila to see what we are experiencing with their goods. There is usually a commonality to what is going wrong, e.g., the buttons aren't sewn on well.

These vendors are so appreciative. They thank us for alerting them to the problem. In almost all cases, they say they will stand behind their merchandise.

Almost all the people who work at the Quality Center are longtime employees who have spent a minimum of five years on the sales floor, so they know exactly what they are looking for.

COMMUNITY INVOLVEMENT

My dad told me that the first 20 years of my business life should be devoted entirely to the business, and I followed that advice. But he also said to do my best in terms of community involvement, to carve out the time because it's important for our business and our family to support our communities.

I ran the King County United Way campaign and have served as president of Seattle Goodwill, Children's Hospital Foundation, and the Downtown Seattle Association. I've been active at the University of Washington in a variety of ways, including being chairman of the Board of Advisors of the Tyee Club, which is a booster club that raises money for the university, with particular emphasis on athletics. (Tyee is a word in the Chinook dialect that means "leader" or anything of high quality.)

My sister, Anne, was recently elected chair of the Tyee Club Board of Advisors. She and her husband, Wayne Gittinger, have been honored by the Tyee Club for their generous efforts in raising money for university athletics.

I have taught classes at the UW Business School as a visiting executive. I've limited my service on corporate boards to what was then First Interstate Bank of Washington and the holding company of First Interstate, Safeco Insurance, and Westin Hotels.

Blake is starting his community involvement a little earlier than I did. He and his wife, Molly, are active in the United Way. Since 2004, they have run the fund-raising campaign for the local Alexis de Tocqueville Society, which is part of United Way, for donors of $10,000 or more.

As a national company, we have encouraged our regional managers to get involved in their communities. In most cases, communities feel that a national company doesn't give the level of attention and contributions that they would like. We want our regional managers to be the Nordstrom headquarters in that community and to be actively involved there.

SEATTLE SEAHAWKS

You might say that buying the Seattle Seahawks was another example of our family's community involvement. In 1974, Lloyd headed a group of Seattle investors who wanted to get an expansion National Football League franchise for our city. The price tag for the entire franchise was $16 million (today, some star players get that much money as a contract-signing bonus). Although the NFL stipulated that one single individual had to be the majority owner, Lloyd persuaded his good friend NFL commissioner Pete Rozelle to designate our family (which held 51 percent of ownership) as the principal owner of the team. Sadly,

Lloyd never got a chance to see the team play. He died on a tennis court in Mexico after an NFL owners' meeting in 1976. Elmer, the last surviving brother, represented the eight family members who shared that 51 percent ownership of the Seahawks. We eventually bought out the five minority non-family owners: Herman Sarkowsky, Ned Skinner, Howard Wright, Lynn Himmelman, and Monty Bean.

We ran the team the way we ran our stores in those days, delegating authority to the people running the team. We felt strongly that many sports teams were mismanaged because the owners' approach was too hands-on. We believed that football decisions should be made by football professionals — general managers John Thompson and Mike McCormack, and coaches Jack Patera and Chuck Knox — and they should be held accountable for those decisions. As owners, we Nordstroms concentrated on the budget and the bottom line.

When Elmer retired, John Nordstrom spent part of his time in the role of managing general partner, which he was particularly well suited for, and he did a bang-up job. Looking back on those days, John said, "I tried to stay out of the newspaper. You never saw me quoted and you never saw my picture in the program. We never mentioned the Nordstrom family. We just stayed underground. We tried to treat the players like we did our employees, and to support those guys. I was in the locker room before and after the games. We wanted to make sure the chemistry was right."

For the most part, owning the Seahawks was a lot of fun, and a pretty good financial investment. We sold out every game in the Kingdome, and the waiting list for season tickets reached 20,000. The team wasn't a significant factor in the managing of our business, but it was a significant factor in our happiness.

Now, things weren't always roses. There was a players' strike, and later we had to part company with our first coach, Jack Patera, and then our first general manager, John Thompson. We wanted to win more. People loved the team, but you could see that the day was coming when fans would be more demanding (although no one was more demanding than we were). We'd have cases of people closing their charge accounts when we'd lose a game. There wasn't a lot of that, but there was enough to make you cringe.

Eventually, it started to lose a little bit of its charm and wasn't as much fun. We could have continued owning the team, but we might have had

Elmer with Pete Rozelle in about 1980.
Rozelle was then commissioner of the NFL.

to neglect this business, which was expanding rapidly in the 1980s. We didn't like being in the public eye, and we also knew that eventually we would have to build a new stadium.

In 1988, we sold the team to Ken Behring, a Northern California developer who we thought was an excellent person to take over the ownership role. Our thinking was that he was a self-made, successful businessman who could relate to the players and their situation, and would put all his resources into creating a winning team. We were disappointed that, as things evolved, Mr. Behring tended to use the team as a provider of capital for him and his other businesses, and tried to move the Seahawks to Southern California, but was stopped by the NFL.

In 1997, my cousin John helped lead the way in encouraging Paul Allen, the cofounder of Microsoft, to buy the team and save it for the Pacific Northwest. In 2006, the team almost won the Super Bowl.

I was asked a number of times if owning the Seahawks took our eye off the ball in terms of running our business. No. We are such sports nuts anyway, we would have talked about them even if we hadn't owned them.

THE FUTURE OF SEATTLE

These days, as I talk to my contemporaries, some of them wring their hands and say that we don't have individuals coming up to lead the city like those in "the good old days." I'm talking about people such as Jim Ellis, Lynn Himmelman, Eddie Carlson, Monty Bean, Dorothy Bullitt, Herman Sarkowsky, Bill Gates Sr. and Mary Gates, Jack Benaroya, Bill Jenkins, Howard Wright, Richard Fuller, and John Ellis (Jim's brother). That's just a sampling of the people who made this city and region what it is today.

I consider Jim Ellis to be the greatest private citizen in the history of Seattle. The list of Jim's accomplishments is a long one. In 1957, he was instrumental in the creation of the Municipality of Metropolitan Seattle, better known as Metro, a municipal corporation run by representatives of King County and local governments that provides the region with waste-treatment facilities, mass transit, and regional parks. Metro cleaned up Lake Washington and reduced water pollution in King County. In 1968, Jim founded the Forward Thrust bond initiatives, which helped build public parks and financed the Kingdome. Under his leadership, in 1976, the city of Seattle completed the construction of Freeway Park, a unique urban space built over Interstate 5 that restored a link between

As long as we keep the headquarters of companies here in Seattle, then we will have the brainpower, initiative, and vision that will drive this region forward.

In 2006, I shared a handshake with Jim Ellis, whom I consider the greatest private citizen in the history of Seattle.

downtown Seattle and First Hill. In 1979, Jim led the way for passage of the $50 million King County Farmland Preservation bond, which enabled the county to buy and preserve farmland and open space. In the 1990s, he founded Mountains to Sound Greenway, which protected a strip of open space along Interstate 90.

I think the people who are wringing their hands, worrying about today's civic leadership, are wrong. We have plenty of people like the ones I cited. We are fortunate that the Bill Gateses of the world are young and have achieved more than anybody could ever possibly imagine. I would also cite people such as Jeff Brotman (Costco), Sally Jewell (REI), Paul Allen (Microsoft), Phyllis Campbell (The Seattle Foundation), Howard Schultz (Starbucks), and Mike McGavick (formerly of Safeco Insurance).

The corporate structure here is certainly different from when I was coming up. Banks used to be known for demanding that their presidents and vice presidents devote a portion of their time to civic ventures because it was good business for them. Today, other than Washington Mutual, Seattle doesn't have any major bank headquarters, which means that we are missing movers and shakers from a significant economic sector. It's the same with retail, as Frederick's and The Bon are no longer here. Now, even Boeing — at least its corporate headquarters — has gone to Chicago.

On the other hand, look at the corporate giants we do have — Microsoft, Costco, Paccar, Safeco, Starbucks, Amazon.com, and, yes, Nordstrom — that are providing the new leadership. As long as we keep the headquarters of companies here in Seattle, then we will have the brainpower, initiative, and vision that will drive this region forward.

THE ACQUISITION OF JEFFREY

For quite a while, we had been aware of Jeffrey Kalinsky and his two luxury Jeffrey boutiques, in Atlanta and New York's Meatpacking District. *Women's Wear Daily*, *Vanity Fair*, and all the publications for fashionistas consider him one of the top fashion-retail gurus in this country. By reputation, I knew of his dad, Morris Kalinsky, who has shoe stores in South Carolina.

My son Pete became more and more curious about this guy, who attracts women from all over the world to his store in New York. Sue Patneaude, who headed our designer business for many years, told Pete that she knew Jeffrey, and the next time she saw Jeffrey, she suggested that he call Pete. A rumor that Neiman's was going to buy Jeffrey sparked the idea that his company might be in play. As it turned out, he already had it in the back of his mind that he wanted a bigger stage.

Jeffrey called Pete and they started this deliberate, mutual evaluation process, during which Pete gained tremendous respect for this young man and the way he ran a store — not just for his reputation in the fashion world. After spending time in Jeffrey's store and watching how he waited on customers, Pete told us that Jeffrey did it better than we did, which is not easy in New York. He has a real way about him at the point of sale.

Pete came up with the idea of creating a partnership and getting him aligned with our company. We ended up buying 51 percent of his company. He continues to run it, while also spending much of his time as our director of designer merchandising, partnering with our merchants to expand our designer business.

Jeffrey started his retail career selling shoes at his dad's store, just like my sons, my cousins, and me. I particularly like a quote of his from an interview in the *Seattle Post-Intelligencer*: "I started on the floor, and if I have ever been able to achieve anything in my life, it was because I started on the floor."

I rank our acquisition of Jeffrey right up there with our finally getting Estée Lauder to sell to us, after our acquisition of Best's Apparel.

Ray started with us, running Human Resources, in 1969, after working at The Bon Marché. He eventually became manager of our old Bellevue Square store, and later our downtown Seattle store. He helped us open 12 stores in six years in Northern California, and eventually became co-chairman of the company.

I have a child who is diabetic, and as a result, my wife, Ardythe, is on the board of the Juvenile Diabetes Research Foundation International, which raises funds for research. In 1983, with the blessings of the third generation of Nordstroms, my wife and I started *Nordstrom Beat the Bridge*, a run–walk event underwritten by the company to benefit JDRF Northwest.

The national JDRF organization has a dinner in New York every year to attract high-profile personalities. They always honor a well-known person, such as Lee Iacocca or Mary Tyler Moore. Ardythe had the idea to invite Mr. Bruce to be the person honored, but he's a low-profile guy so, of course, he graciously declined.

But you don't say no to my wife, who is pretty persistent. Bruce was all for supporting the fund-raising, but he said, "We're not going to honor Bruce Nordstrom. We're going to honor the Nordstrom spirit." So he and some salespeople, and my wife and son and I, attended the dinner. Bruce met the actress Mary Tyler Moore, the honorary national chairman, and posed for pictures with her.

Attending the event was extremely uncomfortable for him, but it was an indication of his loyalty. The Nordstrom family expects a tremendous amount of loyalty from their troops, and I agree with that. But they also reciprocate that loyalty. It doesn't mean that they are soft and easy. To the contrary, they have very high standards, and good for them because had they not, I wouldn't have been able to do what I did when I worked for the company.

JOE FAMOLARE

Joe is one of the great characters in our business. He is a third-generation shoe designer and manufacturer who once designed shoes for Broadway shows and the Bolshoi Ballet, when he worked for Capezio.

I first got to know the Nordstrom family in about 1964, when I was working for a company called Marx & Newman, which made Bandolinos and Amalfis. I would often visit Seattle and meet with Bruce and the whole family, and I got to know Bruce well. He's a straight shooter who says what he thinks, and when he says it, he means it.

When I first left Marx & Newman to sell my own line of shoes, I wasn't succeeding. When I would come to Seattle, Bruce often picked me up at the airport and took me home for dinner, when Blake, Pete, and Erik were little kids. After dinner, he'd drive me back to the hotel. Before I got out of the car, I would say, "Hey, Bruce, I'm seeing your buyers tomorrow. Could you put in a good word for me?" He'd say, "No, I can't do that, Joe. You've got to sell them on your own." You know what? He meant it.

Not too long ago, I got a call from Blake, inviting me to come to Seattle. When I asked him why, he said they just wanted me to come for a visit. I landed in Seattle and there was a car waiting for me. The driver took me to a hotel, where I was put up in a suite. Later that evening, Bruce and Jeannie picked me up to go to dinner, where we were joined by Blake and Molly, and Anne and Wayne Gittinger. Again, I asked them why they wanted me to come to Seattle. They said, "We just want to look at you, Joe. We haven't seen you in a long time."

The next day, at the store, I was met by 50 or 60 shoe executives from the old days. It was then that I realized they were just being nice to me. I was very touched by that.

I told everyone, "When I came out here, I didn't have a clue as to why I was invited. I thought maybe there was an old charge-back that I had forgotten about." Everyone laughed so hard I thought they were going to fall off their chairs.

My sons — Blake, Erik, and Pete — in 1967

My three sons, who all learned the
business here by sweeping floors and
dogging shoes, just as I did, totally
understand our deal — or should
I say *their deal*.

CHAPTER 25

BLAKE, PETE, AND ERIK

My grandpa concluded his autobiography with these words:

I have my sons with their nice families near me. I have so much to be thankful for, as I could never dream in my young days I would ever live to this age and have things so nice as I now have. It gives me a lot of pleasure to go to the store every day and see the success my sons have made in the business.

I feel exactly the same way. As I retire from this company that has been a part of my life for my entire life, I look around and I like what I see.

My three sons, who all learned the business here by sweeping floors and dogging shoes, just as I did, totally understand our deal — or should I say *their deal*. They are absolutely focused on selling stuff, providing customer service, and maintaining our culture. They all have a pride and loyalty to the family and its reputation, and will never do anything to besmirch that reputation; in fact, they want to improve it. At the end of the day, reputation is what you do this for.

They are reminded every day that there is a legacy, a standard, a level of performance that was created by the people who preceded them. They are competitive guys who are not going to let that slide on their watch. They are going to implement their ideas. Then, when they get to be my age, they can look back and say, "On our watch, the company did pretty darn well."

What drives them is what drove me. I'm proud of what my cousins and I did on our watch. Given the size of our company today, no one will ever top our rate of growth when we were running the show. I idolized my grandpa, my dad, and my uncles. I don't want to belittle what they did. I just want to say that on our watch, things got better. I'll bet my sons all say the same thing in their own way: leave it better than you found it.

Blake, Pete, and Erik like each other, and that's the thing I feel best about. I would feel sad if this business caused them to not like each other. Their mother set an example for them. They constantly saw the importance of family, and I think that rubbed off on them.

Erik, Pete, and Blake in 2006

They are not all the same guy, which is part of the charm. But they are as complete and effective a threesome as you could possibly ask for. If you can respect one another, work hard, and add your own individual talent and perspective, then you have the best of all worlds. This takes work because they don't all think the same, and they each bring something different to the table, which is why we think committees can be effective. You don't want everybody in lockstep.

They are absolutely focused on this business. Like many people in Seattle, they own a boat — one boat, which they all share — and they spend a grand total of a week or two each on the boat a year. The boat doesn't get in the way of what they're doing, which is something that I know my dad would approve of. They have simple tastes. Blake drives a Mustang. Pete and Erik both drive Volvos. Pete and Erik both belong to the Seattle Golf Club, but they never play. Golf is a great game to play at some point in your life, but not right now.

Down deep, they are a little competitive with each other, but they also don't want to let the other guy down. They want to achieve and contribute and have the other two guys say, "Nice going."

I can't tell you how rewarding it is for me to hear Blake say, "Pete's got our merchandising operation running on all cylinders. I don't know what we'd do without him."

I'm equally as proud to hear people congratulate Erik on being a terrific leader in the operations of the stores. Erik, who is in the stores more than anybody else, is the expense-control guy, and he gets a lot of accolades for that. On his watch, we now have the lowest percentage of expenses in the modern history of this company.

All three of these men are good communicators with our employees, and by their actions, they have generated respect. They are listened to when they do recognition meetings and communiqués in *The Loop*, which is the employee newsletter. Their words and direction resonate throughout the company.

They are reminded every day that there is a legacy, a standard, a level of performance that was created by the people who preceded them.

RETIREMENT

I'm comfortable with retirement. As long as we're on the course that we're on, with the people who are running it, I couldn't be more pleased.

Now, I'm still going to come down here and enjoy looking over their shoulders, and I'll never tire of looking at merchandise and learning about what's going on in the marketplace, because I'm still a shoe dog at heart. But I'm not going to feel compelled to be here every day as I used to. I'll be a little quieter with my suggestions; I'll be backing off.

Enrique "Rick" Hernandez Jr., who has been a company director since 1997 and the lead director since 2000, became the non-executive chairman of the board when I officially retired in May 2006. Rick, who is president and CEO of Inter-Con Security Systems, Inc., in Pasadena, California, is a good leader who is terrific at running directors' meetings. He serves as a great bridge between inside directors and outside directors, and is able to explain to the outside directors what our management team is doing and why they are doing it.

We are less insular today than we used to be. Of the seven members of our Executive Group, three came from outside the company.

I think it's unlikely that another generation of our family will be as interested as my sons are in running this company. If they are, there are some good candidates among my five grandchildren. My oldest granddaughter, Alexandra, is in high school and gets good grades. She rows on the crew, plays basketball, and is active in many phases of high-school life. Blake and Molly's son, Andy, my oldest grandson, is in eighth grade. He has impressed me with his spirit and how hard he works. Erik and Julie's older daughter, Leigh, who will be going to high school with Alex, has a wonderful talent as a writer. Their third child, Sara, who is still in grade school, has a marvelous spirit and energy. Erik and Julie's son, Sam, is a well-rounded person and a good student, and he seems to turn out for every sport. It'll be exciting to see what the future brings for these kids.

I have often been asked the question "What are you most proud of on your watch?"

My answer is: "We went from a business where every employee knew who I was, and where I knew most every employee — and where there was always a Nordstrom on the floor — to a business where we have

50,000 employees from coast to coast, and most of them don't know me and I don't know them. But the important thing is that we do it better today than we did it years ago."

I think our greatest accomplishment is that the culture has taken on a life of its own.

When I started selling shoes, I was proud to make my draw consistently because I wasn't a very good salesman. To make the draw I had to sell 180 dollars' worth of shoes a day, at a time when the typical shoe retailed for less than 10 dollars a pair. I didn't want people to think I was just hanging on because I was the boss's son. So I'm not kidding when I say that making my draw was a big, big deal for me.

When I became a department manager, and later a store manager, and I had relatively good numbers, I was proud of that, too.

I'm proud of the recognition we got when we went from a shoe store to the store we became. There were so many naysayers. We moved into a new business (apparel) and accelerated the growth of the company. We took over the business from our dads and took the company public. I was the one who had to speak to the investment community and analysts, and was able to communicate our way of doing things. As you might imagine, that has been very gratifying for me.

I'm proud of — and humbled by — the fact that every year we are selected as one of the top companies to work for in America. In 2006, we were rated as the most admired general merchandise retailer in a survey by *Fortune* magazine.

If my grandpa came back today and saw this company, it would boggle his mind. He was overwhelmed when our annual sales reached $1 million. (In 2005, we had sales of $7.9 billion.)

If my dad came back today and saw this business, he would be proud. I'm not sure he would tell me he was proud, but I know he would be.

I have finished up my time with our company feeling that the last years were the most rewarding I've ever had in this business.

All in all, I think we did pretty good. I'm proud to say that we left it better than we found it.

My wonderful family, holiday 2005

AUTHOR'S NOTE

There are countless people who have enriched my life, both personally and professionally. I wish I could have named them all in the book. In lieu of that, I would like to give everyone thanks for their hard work and efforts to make Nordstrom one of the world's finest stores. We literally could not have done it without you.

I'd also like to thank all of my executive assistants over these past years. I am eternally grateful for their support.

Kathryn Gagnon

Karen Purpur

Carolee Schiersh

Kathy Suznevich

Esther Thomas

I would also like to thank Robert Spector for his assistance with the writing of this book, and his unflagging encouragement.

Our staff did an excellent job of fact-checking this book, and their invaluable efforts were led by Paula Weigand and Brooke White.

NORDSTROM HISTORICAL TIMELINE

1901 Wallin & Nordstrom open their first shoe store in Seattle. First-day sales are $12.50.

1923 Wallin & Nordstrom open their second store, in Seattle's University District.

1928 John W. Nordstrom retires and sells his share of the company to his sons Everett and Elmer.

1929 Carl Wallin sells his share of the business to the Nordstrom family.

October 29, "Black Tuesday," signals the crash of the stock market and the beginning of the Great Depression.

1930 With the grand opening of an expanded Second Avenue store, Wallin & Nordstrom becomes Nordstrom's.

1933 Lloyd Nordstrom joins his older brothers in the business.

1937 Nordstrom moves its downtown store from Second Avenue to Fifth and Pike, where it will remain for the next 61 years.

1941 The United States enters World War II with the bombing of Pearl Harbor. Despite challenges brought on by shoe rationing, Nordstrom emerges from the war years stronger and more vital.

1950 Nordstrom opens its first suburban store, just north of Seattle at Northgate, considered to be one of the first shopping malls in the country.

The company also opens its first store in downtown Portland.

1958 Nordstrom opens its Bellevue store.

1959 Nordstrom is known as the largest independently owned shoe store in the United States, with over 100,000 pairs of shoes in stock.

1963 Nordstrom acquires Best's Apparel and enters the apparel business.

Bruce Nordstrom is named president of the company.

1968 The third generation of the Nordstrom family — cousins Bruce, Jim, and John, and Jack McMillan — take over the leadership of the company.

1969 Nordstrom changes its name to Nordstrom Best.

1971 Nordstrom Best goes public with its first stock offering.

1973   The downtown Seattle store, at Fifth and Pike, undergoes an $11 million expansion. The company also changes its name to Nordstrom, Inc.

Company sales surpass the $100 million mark.

1975   The Nordstrom Rack opens on the lower level of the downtown store as a clearance center for full-line store merchandise.

1978   Nordstrom opens its first store in California, at South Coast Plaza.

1985   Annual sales for Nordstrom, Inc., surpass $1 billion.

1988   The first East Coast store opens, at Tysons Corner Center in McLean, Virginia.

1989   Nordstrom and French apparel company Façonnable sign a U.S. licensing agreement.

1990   The first Northeast store opens, in Paramus, New Jersey.

1991   The first Midwest store opens, in Oak Brook, Illinois.

1993   Nordstrom Direct is launched, offering customers the opportunity to shop by catalog.

1995   The third generation retires from day-to-day management of the company; they remain on the board of directors. Six members of the fourth generation become co-presidents.

1996   The first Texas store opens, at the Dallas Galleria.

1998   The new flagship store opens in the renovated Frederick & Nelson building in downtown Seattle. That same year, the company launches Nordstrom.com.

Company sales exceed $5 billion.

2000   Blake Nordstrom is named president of the company. Bruce Nordstrom comes out of retirement to become chairman of the board.

The company also acquires Façonnable.

2001   Nordstrom celebrates its 100th year in business.

2004   Jack McMillan retires from the board of directors.

2005   Nordstrom acquires a majority interest in Jeffrey specialty stores.

2006   Bruce Nordstrom and John Nordstrom retire from the board of directors.

Company sales for the year exceed $8.5 billion.

INDEX